CRUCIBLE

of

SHAME

HEALING THE SOCIETAL ROOTS
OF ADDICTION AND "MENTAL ILLNESS"

STEFAN J. MALECEK, PH. D.

CRUCIBLE OF SHAME

HEALING THE SOCIETAL ROOTS OF ADDICTION AND "MENTAL ILLNESS"

Stefan J. Malecek, Ph. D.

COPYRIGHT

Stefan J. Malecek, Ph.D.

DISCLAIMER

The author of this book does not dispense medical advice or prescribe the use of any technique as a form of treatment for physical, emotional or medical problems without the advice of a physician either directly or indirectly. The author is only sharing information of a general nature to help you in your quest for your emotional, physical or spiritual wellbeing.

What I bring to the table is almost 4 decades of studying the effects of shame and treating trauma and mental illness survivors in individual and group settings. What I describe here is a multidimensional approach to understanding the effects of shame and the root causes of addiction and mental illness based on what I have seen work on my patients, my loved ones and myself. In the event that you use the information in this book for yourself, the author assumes no responsibilities for your actions.

TABLE OF CONTENTS

Copyright i

Disclaimer ii

Get A Free Copy Of: Trauma And Transformation 1

Other Books By Stefan J. Malecek, Ph.D 2

Dedication 3

Preface To Book One 4

Chapter One: From The Beginning.. 5

   Circle Of Life... 5

   Birth Trauma.. 6

   Creation 7

   The Self.. 7

   The False Self 8

   Attachment And Self 10

   Disorganized Attachment 13

   Self-Image 14

Chapter Two: Emotion.. 17

   Definition... 17

   Stages Of Emotional Development 18

   Affect... 19

   Affect Hunger 19

   External Focus 20

   Brain Models 21

   Model Imperative... 21

Chapter Three: Shame 23

   Definition... 23

Categories Of Shame 24

Caustic Cycle Of Shame 25

Systemic Shame 26

Autonomy Vs. Shame 28

Shame And The Diminution Of The Sacred 29

Shamed Desire 30

Self-Repudiation 31

Delusion 32

Woundedness 33

Chapter Four: Shame-Based Childrearing 35

Disrupted Development 35

Shame And Codependence 36

Children As Commodities 37

Some Political Considerations 39

Chapter Five: Trauma 41

The Biochemistry Of Trauma 41

Traumatic Bonding 43

Triggers 43

Flashbacks 44

Chapter Six: Dissociation 47

Definition 47

Etiology 48

Dissociation And The False Self 49

Projection 49

Multiplicity Or Multidimensionality? 52

Chapter Seven: Addictions Part I 54

Definition 54

Etiology 55

Medical Model..57

Brief Critique Of The Medical Model 58

Free Will Model...59

Addiction As Delusion 60

Addiction And Dissociation 61

Chapter Eight: Addictions Part II..62

"Authorizing" Addictions...62

A Plug For Drugs...63

Suppression Of Altered States..64

War On Drugs, Or War Against People?....................................67

A Small Personal Story..69

Aftermath..72

Chapter Nine: Scarcity And Social Darwinism..........................74

Enough...74

Belief And "Reality"..75

Social Darwinism..77

Ideology 79

Ideological Hegemony..81

Chapter Ten: The Culture Of Greed 83

Definition..83

Greed And The False Self..84

Greed And Acquisition...85

Shopping...86

Greed And Violence 87

Chapter Eleven: Societal Structure..89

Shaping The Container 89

Advertising And Ideology 91

Impression Management..95

Other Artifacts Of Socialization 97

Television And Violence 98

The Most Recent Statistics...100

Chapter Twelve: The Corporate State Part I...........................103

The Etiology Of The Corporate State 103

In Pre-Columbian Days..104

Ancient Roots 105

Sociopathy And The East India Corporation (Eic) 106

The World Of Time 108

Chapter Thirteen: Corporate State Part II 110

Original Intentions 110

First And Fourth Amendments 112

The Fourteenth Amendment 113

Corporate Manipulation..114

The King Of Spectacle Politics...116

Cultural Collusion And The Juristic Person 118

The Prison Industry...119

Chapter Fourteen: Corporatizing Addictions 120

Creating Addictions 120

The Unethical Empire..122

Technology And Excitement Addiction 123

Chapter Fifteen: The Birth Of Corporate Psychiatry 125

Descartes' Legacy...125

Fateful Folly..128

The "Normal" Stance 129

Power And Authority...130

Law And Psychiatry..132

Chapter Sixteen: Selling "Mental Illness" 135

Preface 135

Community Mental Health Centers (Cmhc)........................... 137

Still No Proof... 138

Chapter Seventeen: War And The Permanent War

Economy 141

Projection And War 142

Shame And War... 144

Martial Conditioning 145

The Permanent War Economy.. 146

Projection And Politics 148

Media And A Taste Of History 150

War As Addiction.. 152

Healing And The Permanent War Economy 153

Book Two.. 155

Chapter Eighteen: Ways And Means................................. 155

Some Personal Reflections 155

Preface For Book Two.. 155

Shame As Potentially Beneficial 156

Alone Or Lonely? 157

Adversity 159

Challenge 160

Overwhelm 162

Introspection And Inspiration 163

There Is No Success Like Failure... 164

Chapter Nineteen: A Different Way................................. 166

Historical Perspective 166

Some Famous Examples... 167

Forgiveness, Mourning, And Creative Expression.................. 168

Forgiveness And Recovery 170

The Next Larger View 172

Chapter Twenty: Beyond Cultural Norms And Forms 174

Authenticity And The Self..174

Transformation And The Alchemy Of Art 176

Abreaction And Catharsis..176

The Importance Of Transformative Tears 177

Writing 179

Like A Hero's Journey...180

Cultural Revolution...182

Cooperation, Not Competition...184

The Possibility Of An Ecstatic Society....................................186

Job Vs. Work 188

A Partial (And Incomplete) View 189

Joy Is Our Birthright 191

About The Author. 192

References 194

GET A FREE COPY OF:

TRAUMA AND TRANSFORMATION

Your Free Book Is Waiting

During a lifetime, everyone takes on the burden of unexpressed emotions, regrets and missed opportunities around which may develop a kind of psychic scar tissue which might eventually lead to emotional and psychological trauma. This book functions as a road map to help you understand better the effects of trauma, recovery from trauma and dealing with addiction and mental illness. The author draws upon his own life experiences and research garnered from over fifty years of working in the mental health industry to show that healthy expression of these suppressed injuries is perhaps the only path to true mental health recovery.

OTHER BOOKS BY STEFAN J. MALECEK, PH. D

Crucible of Shame: Healing the Societal Roots of Addiction and "Mental Illness"

Trauma And Transformation (Read For Free)

The Paul Marzeky Mystery Series

Crazy Tales of Combat Psychiatry

Spirals of Time

Unwitting Witnesses

Alchemy's Angel

The Gilded Edges of Shadow

Excelsior

DEDICATION

Writing is a lonely business. No writer works in a complete vacuum. I have been vastly assisted during my journey both as a person and a writer by so many people who have contributed to enriching my life in many ways. I am grateful to them

PREFACE TO BOOK ONE

THE CRUCIBLE OF SHAME: HEALING THE SOCIETAL ROOTS OF ADDICTION AND "MENTAL ILLNESS"

Even if you cannot define it; even if you cannot describe it—you have experienced shame. "Let us not forget that small emotions are the great captains of our lives and that we obey them without knowing it" once said Vincent Van Gogh.

Everyone gets shamed some time in their lives. Most of us do not remember the earliest incidents. Almost every adult remembers times when he or she one has been shamed. There is a reason for that.

The import of shame is so strong that one does not usually remember early experiences of it because it is too painful. The younger the child, the more powerful the memory. Since all memory is encoded and recalled based on emotional intensity, this makes perfect sense. Babies are almost pure emotion. Therefore, it makes perfect sense that one neither remembers nor wishes to remember one's earliest shaming experiences. Why would one want to do so?

Before I further investigate this important question and explicate some avenues for healing shame, I will first define exactly what shame is and how it acts upon the tender human nervous system.

CHAPTER ONE
FROM THE BEGINNING

Unlike most other species, we are not biologically programmed to know what to do; rather we are an experiment in free choice. This leaves us with an enormous potential, powerful egotism, and tremendous anxiety

Sahtouris, 1989, p. 24.

The successful joining of a sperm cell and an egg creating a fetus also contain the hopes and dreams, fears and shame, desires and aspirations of his or her parents. Kotulaki noted that "At eight months, a baby's brain has about 1000 trillion connections, and is growing at the incredible rate of three billion a second."

Since the newborn is extremely sensitive to every energetic impulse, it is no wonder that a child exhibits irritability, pain, crying jags, "temper tantrums," and the desire to sleep a great deal.

Circle of Life

Morowitzii beautifully explicated the process of consciousness arising:

First, the human mind, including consciousness and reflective thought, can be explained by activities of the central nervous system, which, in turn, can be reduced to the biological structure and

5

function of that physiological system.

Second, biological phenomena at all levels can be totally understood in terms of atomic physics, that is, through the action and interaction of the component atoms of carbon, nitrogen, oxygen, and so forth.

Third and last, atomic physics, which is now understood most fully by means of quantum mechanics, must be formulated with the mind as a primitive component of the system.

Birth Trauma

Numerous researchers have debunked the false belief that the newborns do not feel pain. Meade commented that "We come with a wound that is exacerbated by childhood."iii. Freudiv early postulated that birth was the first experience of terror and anxiety. When Rankv set out to identify "the ultimate biological basis of the psychical…the very nucleus of the unconscious," he proclaimed that birth was the root of all traumatic experience. Imagine how terribly shocking and painful it must be, coming out of the water-world of the womb where one has been exquisitely catered to, and suddenly having to breathe air, all alone and defenseless in a hostile Universe—initiating the sense of exclusion or disconnection from others, and may also plant the seed of desire to find comfort and satisfaction in experiences external to the self.

Creation

No one creates the world into which he or she is born. The parents' desire and choice to give a newborn child "the very best" is colored by their own life experiences and shaped by the pre-existing society with the tenets of diverse cultures, dreams and visions, rules and regulations. A newborn's parents act in aegis for the entire of society, providing the initial norms and boundaries around which a child grows, modeling for the newborn the "natural" patterns of association or dislocation embodied by his or her parent's society with its principles and assumptions, and passed along unexamined vi—passing along the void of hunger for human connection to yet another generation.

He further noted that such habitual, automatized shaping may, in fact, be considered to be desirable from a societal point of view as it may tend to influence an individual to be more easily absorbed into adopting the culturally and or societally "proper" perceptions, and therefore act in ways that are congruent with the promoted and "authorized" points of view and behaviors.

The Self

The self is a "social creation."vii It develops interactively as an organizing principle that requires feedback from the social environment.viii Selfness and "ego" ix may be seen as emblematic of the awareness of separation created at birth and incrementally as one becomes an increasingly isolated yet "functional" individual, though, as Krishnamurti once elegantly commented "It is no measure of good health to be well adjusted to a profoundly sick society."

"Each person, through the ability to symbolize experience, carries internal representations of their real social world" and become a personal model of self.x The sense of self is grounded in the mirroring eyes of others, reflecting joy, pain, sorrow and happinessxi. It is, in this sense, "allowed" by others"xii. As an infant, the affect-laden examples of the caregivers are absorbed completely and without critical judgment. "Self-feeling is simply the certainty that the feelings and wishes one experiences are a part of one's self...This natural contact with one's own emotions and wishes is what gives one a sense of strength and esteem."xiii

The False Self

Winnicott xiv created the concept of the false self to describe the process of an individual's unconsciously developing a mask or persona to wear in order to hide his or her true and authentic self. If one is not mirrored and echoed adequately by those whose task it was to reflect attention back to the child his or her attempts at speech and emotions, one may develop a deficit in self-expression, driven by a negative evaluation not only of oneself, but of the world. "Since one feels his true self is defective and flawed, one needs a false self that is not defective and flawed. Once one becomes a false self, one ceases to exist psychologically. To be a false self is to cease being an authentic human being."xv

What we take for granted as "reality" is actually far more complex. Because of assumed automaticity (expectations we all assume are shared) the everyday construction of personal experience may easily become dulled because one stops paying attention. Most of us are lulled into the stupor of "normal" consciousness. Automaticity then develops, and thereinafter it is only the brain's "constructions and simulations" of which one may be aware. Consciousness is reduced to a state of "partly suspended animation and inability to function, a daze, a stupor...A state of profound abstraction, a great retreat from immediate sensory/instinctual reality to abstraction about reality." xvi

A child may accommodate the impact of a traumatic situation by imposing on his or herself a "false sense of order on the disorder [by] the repudiation of childhood needs and the disruption of childhood beliefs."xvii

Every child needs unconditional love. Failing to get it from one's caregivers may condition the child (through the process of internalizing a negative self-evaluation) to develop poor self-esteem, depression, phobias, and a host of other physical symptoms, such as failure to thrive syndrome, in which a child may actually die from lack of loving care and attention. Denial of the injury is followed by a further separation within oneself, a lessened feeling of embodiment (known as dissociation that I will discuss further in greater detail in a later chapter) that momentarily lessens both the traumatic impact and one's awareness. This then warps how an individual both frames the injury and how an individual thereinafter creates a kind of alternate reality through which one attempts to "function" in spite of the now-internalized traumatic import.

Everyone is left hungering for wholeness. The experience of unconditional love is like a neurological imprint of safety and personal worthiness. It is impossible for anyone to get enough. No one has perfect parents. To experience unconditional love from birth might be akin to being enlightened, in that there would be no barriers to the direct perception of the unvarnished energy of the Universe and no fear of experiencing it (or so I am told).

These early positive nurturing experiences deeply influence what becomes the core of one's "personality," that grows with increasing life experience, shaped to a large extent by the container of society.

Most people develop acceptable self-images by accommodating their values to the logic of their activities, which are in turn structured by society's institutional boundary…therefore, powerful pressures push people to seek only what society is prepared to bestow upon them. xviii

Attachment and Self

One's mother (Greek, "origin") has a tremendous influence, especially while the fetus is in her womb. Her choice of foods, medicines, and other drugs all affect the growing zygote. Any mood-altering drugs have the possibility of mutating the growing child. The fetus is incredibly emotionally vulnerable, easily imprinted with the tone of his or her earliest lessons, like black ink on the white paper of consciousness.

Failing to respond to signs of distress in the child may "eventuate in a corresponding detachment in the child. The child's reactive detachment sets the stage for reliance on dissociation as a response to 'active abuse.'" xix

Mothers shape the nature of a child's personality far more than any other factor. An individual develops and matures in the framework of this most-trusted person's ideas, beliefs and actions that then lead the individual to create a personal reality. It is the lens through which one filters and views the events and experiences of one's life. This is nurtured by the need of the developing child's brain to attune to the mother's brain to establish stability; and acquire personal boundaries, models for self-definition, and self-expression that lead to a sense of being recognized and held valuable. (This is established with the child's need to be held and comforted, attuning his or her brain waves and heartbeat to the mother's). These are internalized directly and form the basis of one's "reality."

"Reality" is the term most often to describe what is actually "naïve reality," by which any individual names his or her personal perceptual awareness "reality," while really only referring to his or her own experience. This also related to what I have called "personal fascism." As one presents one's false self to the world, one creates a pervasive "character defect," based on wanting to please significant adults in order to feel loved and valued, even if one's distorted personal views are completely correct. In this instance, one then acts as if the world should run according to one's own standards, and perfectly meet one's idiosyncratic needs and wishes. (This may, in fact, be delusional).

Attachment behavior is the infant's natural inclination to turn toward one's mother for nurture and protection. Infants and young children eagerly seek an adult response, as their neurons awaken to a call-and-respond process to "other." xx The manner and depth with which any infant attaches to his or her caregiver is regulated by internalizing the feeling-tones of the caregiver (e.g., soft, gentle, harsh, painful). By definition, any stressor will be an impetus for a developing infant or child to seek closer proximity to the caregiver, and will affect an individual's attachment style, xxi xxii, xxiii.

Forming a secure attachment develops a foundation for which there is no substitute. The failure to develop a secure attachment may create an organic sense of deficit, and lead to one becoming his or her own internalized perpetrator as a result of disowning or repudiating one's self—in much the same manner as a building foundation constructed with faulty materials.

The child's recognition of the presence (or absence) of the caregiver, and his or her behaviors, role models future relationships. This experience predicates one's ability to successfully predict the behaviors of, and develop relationships with, others. Inconsistent role-modeling (e.g., enduring the mother's vacillating or fluctuating moods); or being a child with physical problems (e.g., colic), may override the child's ability to adequately internalize, perhaps even reject, the caregiver's efforts.

The process of internalizing abuse results from the desperate need to maintain a relationship, even a destructive one." xxiv "Under conditions of abuse, neglect, or gross insensitivity, an inordinate degree of self-sufficiency is required of the young child." xxv This may develop into a generalized fear of vulnerability, even to developing a phobia of attachment as being filled with the potential for harm.

Disorganized Attachment

Blizardxxvi framed dissociation as an individual's attempt to manage distorted emotional input from attachment figures that arises when a child cannot create a secure attachment because of feeling unsafe. It will disrupt the normal process of the child seeking safety from the caregiver, wherein the child can neither approach the caregiver, flee nor shift attention to the environment. This disorganized attachment may eventually lead to an attraction to illusion-creating addictions in a vain attempt to simulate the sense of wholeness lost or disturbed by trauma.

Frightening or sexualized behavior toward the infant; disorganized or disoriented behaviors in response to the infant's needs; or deferential role-inversion (in which a mother seeks her own comfort from, instead of giving to, the infant), all may lead to disorganized behavior. "The child's needs for soothing and attachment…may be subjugated to the parents' fear of attachment or need for control," and may lead to dissociative adaptation to protect the self "from being vulnerable to exploitation." xxvii

"Environmental failure triggers traumatic memory which evokes traumatic affect which leads to the possibility of some kind of addictive activity." Disorganization serves to keep information that "must be unnoticed, disallowed, unacknowledged, or forgotten," separated in consciousness. xxviii All of this allows for the propagation of an altered or dissociative state which keeps deflected— "that which one dares not experience," while "allowing the individual to access the needs embedded in the split-off parts of the self." xxix

The only recourse a baby has when his screams are ignored is to repress his distress, which is tantamount to mutilating his soul, for the result is an interference with his ability to feel, to be aware, and to remember...because those torments, together with the needs related to them [will be] ... completely banished from consciousness. xxx

Self-Image

An infant begins life by being a profligate "taster," with everything initially going in the mouth. That leads to the child developing a menu for that which tastes "good," and a sense of having an "inside" that is distinct from his or her "outside." The child is repeatedly given a name with which he or she comes to identify and to respond. Internalizing both positive and negative emotions facilitates the emergence of shame, that Tomkinsxxxi demonstrated was inborn.

From these reflections, one creates a positive or negative sense of selfhood, and begins to utilize the "I" pronoun to differentiate between self and others. This new pronoun replaces "me" in the vocabulary of most children around the age of three, reflecting a sufficient level of stored life experience to shed the magical thinking of earliest childhood.

This contributes to the model of self-care a child adopts, one that may remain relatively stable throughout the child's life. The organization of the emerging child's personality is surely impacted. The manner and quality in which one is treated

will be absorbed without discrimination, since the brain of the developing child is extremely plastic and impressionable xxxii xxxiii

This plasticized brain learning of infancy and earliest childhood is called neoteny. xxxiv Poorly internalized role models lead to a poor self-image. If, during these primary and critical interactions, one feels loved and valued, one's brain will become attuned to positive energies and develop a sense of competence, efficacy, and value. If, conversely, one incorporates predominately negative early experiences as the foundation of self, and internalizes them as if they were one's own, one may develop an amplified negative self-image, exhibiting self-destructive or other violent behaviors, and acting on them as if such judgments were actually valid and deserved.

Everyone develops some measure of competency, hardiness, and self-sufficiency, despite one's foundational experiences of self, and the creation of a potentially untenable self-image. Symptoms of "mental illness" are also an adaptation, albeit dysfunctional. In any case, critical examination remains necessary as one grows, and more deeply and efficiently attempts to manage the changing scenery of one's life, attempting to maximize healthy self-care.

CHAPTER TWO

EMOTION

Emotions are complex, subjective experiences that have many components, including physical, expressive, cognitive and organizing, as well as highly personalize meanings....[That] help to define and organize all experiences.

Greenspan & Greenspan, 1985, p. 7.

Definition

Whereas visual perception is about how we see the outside world; [and] whereas a feeling of thirst is about the inner world, emotions are different. They mediate between inner and outer worlds." xxxv "The security in one's own capacity for regulation…is a fundamental ability that is at the very foundation of human emotional experience." xxxvi Learning to recognize, evaluate, and embody self-soothing techniques is the primary task of mid- to late infancy.

The emotions function to organize the brain; to prepare mechanisms of action and bodily resources; to direct attention; to set up biases of cognitive processing; and to amplify the import of the issue that caused the emotion and make it salient in consciousness." The felt-experience of this signal is a distinctive feeling of happiness, sadness, anger, or some other emotional state." xxxvii

Stages of Emotional Development

The three major needs of children are: being validated (mirrored) by significant others; being able to identify with competent people; to gain a sense of belonging by seeing similarities with others. xxxviii

Greenspan and Greenspan xxxix asserted that the ability of a child to learn to self-soothe was the primary wellspring of emotional health that assured an individual of a solid platform upon which to navigate the inevitable turmoil of everyday life. Additionally, they set briefly described six essential developmental milestones of emotional growth in infants.

To feel tranquil in spite of multitudinous sense impressions and to reach out actively for them.

To take a highly specialized interest in the human world.

To enter a dialogue with one's parents; to learn to connect small units of feeling and social behavior into large, complicated, orchestrated patterns.

To learn to go from understanding how objects function to being able to create these objects in one's mind's eye.

To expand one's world of ideas into the emotional realms of pleasure and dependency, curiosity, empathy and love.

To have an emotional dialogue, to communicate emotions...that grows into the desire to interact in ever more complicated ways...and eventually to the ability to construct an internal life, that is, to imagine experiences for oneself."

Affect

Humans experience affect as physiological phenomenon amplified by awareness and revealed as consciousnessxl. Affect is biology, while emotion is biography. Nathansonxli noted that "Affect is the link between need, its identification, and its later relief, that allows us to grow into adulthood trusting our emotions as an important source of information."

Affect Hunger

Affect hunger is "The incessant and insatiable seeking of affection" xlii that develops as a result of an insecure attachment. It manifests as a craving for self-soothing, and to preserve one's sense of self from "total ego annihilation, using the very same maladaptive coping skills and interpersonal styles of communicating and relating, enmeshed and without boundaries, with which one had been reared."xliii Aggression, impulsiveness, and low frustration tolerance are likely artifacts of this.

Psychosomatic diseases of all sorts (i.e., asthma, lupus erythematosus, etc.) may appear in children whose mothers "remain fused in a highly pathological nexus, with the baby fulfilling many of the mother's needs for care, warmth and attachment... with the child fulfilling the function of an addictive object." xliv

A need for self-aggrandizement may also develop as a sequel of pathological patterns that suppress healthy self-love.

Often individuals with mirror hungry personalities experience tremendous "narcissistic rage" episodes when their immediate needs aren't met—they experience any rejection as a threat to their sense of self and respond by attacking the source of danger. Underneath all this is the lingering risk of empty depression that reflects the sense of non-being so dangerous to those whose needs for mirroring have not been adequately met. xlv

Affect hunger may also account for the well-known phenomenon of "trading addictions" (e.g., quitting heroin and becoming an alcoholic) because the underlying core emotional hunger has not been satisfied.

External Focus

Around the age of three, the child begins to differentiate between self and other; to more deeply recognize that he or she is not the center of the Universe; and to begin to grasp the complexity of the unexplored world beyond the senses. The child begins to develop an increasingly externalized focus around this time, attempting to fulfill arising inner longings. Shame-based childrearing methods inculcate the loss of autonomy in generation after generation of children.

Touting continually increasing production and consumption of goods and services is a vainglorious attempt to stanch the inner emptiness that is in keeping with the dissociative nature of contemporary society.

Brain Models

The Newtonian-Cartesian model of the brain dominated science for over four hundred years, characterizing it as a clockwork mechanism, with gears meshing (or failing to do so); and of which each individual was a part of the Great Machine of the Universe. Then the computer model became the mainstay of scientific modeling.

Later, Talbot proposed a Holographic Model that delineated a matrix of connections between each and every brain, and the Universe as a whole that operates through it. Therefore, the brain is only a receptor of, and amplifier for, these larger, more complex impulses. xlvi

Model Imperative

Pearcexlvii noted that Nature's exquisite bounty is utilized to "Determine to an indeterminable extent the character, nature, and quality of the new intelligence that manifests." He called this "model imperative," and applied it to the birth of any newborn. When he compared two groups of pregnant rat mothers, he found that

Subjected to a hostile, competitive, anxiety-producing environment, she will give birth to an infant with an enlarged hindbrain, an enlarged body and musculature, and a reduced forebrain...If the mother is in a secure, harmonious, stress-free, nurturing environment during gestation, she will produce an infant with an enlarged forebrain, reduced hindbrain, and smaller body.

His work emphasizes emotional influence even in utero, especially the development of an enhanced limbic system created for dealing more effectively with the possibility of a hostile environment at birth. He noted that the amygdala mediates memory, regulates the stress response, and integrates information (including emotions, and environmental cues from memory). After initially being stored in the neocortex, research has determined that the hippocampus is the primary long-term storage facility for memory. xlviii,xlix

CHAPTER THREE

SHAME

The way we exist in the element of shame is as difficult for us to perceive as it is for a fish to know the water they live in or birds the air they breathe

Kilbourne, 1992, p. 224.

Definition

The word shame is derived from Proto-Indo-European (PIE), meaning "to cover" (covering oneself being a common expression of shame). The word has commonly come to be used in the negative sense, relating to diminution of one's self-perception in some manner, as distinguished from guilt.

"The experience of shame is directly about the self, which is the focus of [negative] evaluation. In guilt, the self is negatively evaluated in connection with something, but is not itself the focus of the experience." 1 Lyndli described it as the unwanted, and frequently unexpected or sudden sense of exposure, of an intense feeling of inadequacy; or a profound sense of not being worthy of love; or a sense of alienation or dislocation. As guilt invites confession and forgiveness, shame generates concealment out of a fear of rendering the self to be unacceptable. More importantly even, "Experiences of shame may call into question, not only one's own adequacy and the validity of the codes of one's immediate society, but the meaning of the universe itself."lii

Shame is "The last emotion to be studied by psychiatry, psychology, and all of the psychotherapies"liii but it is for me the most significant and pervasive artifact of the entire human experience. I believe that shame is the master emotion because, "as it is internalized all other emotions are bound to it." Shame is the "pivotal human emotion in monitoring, maintaining, repairing, and developing our inner world of values and the social structures we create to support and give meaning to our lives. It is pre-eminently the social emotion."liv

Categories of Shame

According to Nathanson, there are eight categories of shame. One might feel oneself as deficient in terms of: personal size, strength, ability, skill; helplessness; a loser in competition with others; ugly, deformed, or unattractive; sexually; wishing to avoid being seen by others; unlovable and wishing to be alone." lv

These categories are "Suggestive of patterns of cognitive response…seemingly without awareness of the cultural pathology within which the experience is located."lvi

The proximal cause, initiating impulse, of shame is often someone with whom one has had a strong emotional connection. This impulse may be factual (e.g., one is smaller, slower, et cetera), or a projection of the other. In either case, one is affected by the import of the shaming impulse and internalizes it as if it were "real," and begins to act as if one were damaged, not simply being judged by another's malignant standards. One may then repudiate oneself, using that shame against oneself—and become one's own perpetrator.

The more severe has been the shaming, the more extensive and pervasive the possibility of self-harm. Having been severely shamed, one might easily internalize a shamed self-image that may also perpetuate the Caustic Cycle of Shame.

Caustic Cycle of Shame

Denial of one's own reality. When one is shamed, the bond of trust is shattered. One questions one's own feelings and judgment; and may subsequently withdraw from belief in one's own perceptions (e.g., "Your daddy didn't really mean to hit you. It was an accident").

Confusion and doubt. Simultaneous with one's denial, one necessarily feels confusion and doubt about oneself as a perceiver.

Submission. When repeated lies, slurs, curses and other forms of repudiation are internalized, one may come to accept them and one's innate unworthiness as negative evaluations that are "true."

Being shamed for wanting to have one's own reality. Children may be further shamed when they express any truth that an important adult figure wishes to suppress, or not acknowledge; or that is incongruent with the image the adult wishes the child to believe or express (e.g., "Your mommy isn't drunk. She's sick").

Introjection. Having internalized lies and untruths, one may then begin to believe that harming oneself is protecting oneself (e.g., cutting and other self-harming; or losing is winning, to please or placate the other).

Projection of shame/blame. One may learn to project one's shame onto others in an attempt to manage overwhelming negativity. This may take the form of identifying with the negative aspects of those who have shamed one; or aggression against others who are perceived as weaker, and thus shaming others. This is related to what Ferenczilvii called "identification with the aggressor." Thus, the cycle comes full circle.lviii

Systemic Shame

We live in an addictive system that has embraced institutionalized shame, both as avoidant of human feelings and to kindle addictive behaviors that can be capitalized. Western society as having been founded, and continuing to operate upon, hierarchical principles that embrace control as a central feature, "molding" people away from their natural instincts and creating emotional disconnection. lix

Infant slaughter and abuse have long been a standard,lx one that contemporary people would look upon with horror. Yet so called "modern" childrearing practices embrace cruelty and extensive abuse.lxi Boundary violations are widespread, inevitably leading to a loss of sovereignty and autonomy. As children we have "No history standing in our way, and our tolerance of our parents knows no bounds. The love a child has for his or her parents ensures that their conscious or unconscious acts of mental cruelty will go unnoticed."lxii

Parents regularly use shame to create obedience in their children. It becomes the easiest and most available tool to "correct" behaviors. When a child is shamed often enough, shame may become toxic. The child may begin to adopt a devalued sense of self, as a result of inappropriate words or touch, illicit sexual contact; beatings (often couched as punishment for "wrongdoing"); incessant scolding; brutalizing ridicule; repetitive religious preaching; enforced duties (such as chores for which one might be graded and "punished" for less than perfect completion); even repeated "minor" boundary intrusions (e.g., walking into a child's room without knocking).

Because a child's survival is intricately predicated on the relative stability of the family structure—and important survival figures' behaviors cannot be predicted (or appeased), the child may suffer greatly, even die metaphorically. The child thus becomes a prisoner of childhood. lxiii

Autonomy vs. Shame

Autonomy versus shame and doubt is the second developmental stage of Erikson's taxonomy. It contains a number "Of highly conflicting action patterns characterized by the tendencies of holding on and letting go [wherein] the still highly dependent child begins to experience his autonomous will." lxiv The relationship between a child and his or her parents contains an inherent power differential that lends an aura of violence to childrearing because the parental figures view themselves as authorities. As such they very likely believe that they must be obeyed and "The child becomes a machine which must be set and tuned, even as before it was an animal which must be broken."

Any act of caregiving is conditional upon the needs and desires of one's caregivers. It is almost impossible to not simply see a newborn as both an extension of one's own life, and an opportunity to relive it in a different way. Therefore, to project one's own unmet needs and desires onto the child and wish to see them lived is almost natural for individuals who themselves never had their own developmental needs met appropriately. (As I have discussed, this embraces almost everyone in contemporary society). Healthy families tend to rear healthy children; violent and abusive families tend to rear children in their own image. In this form of automaticity, everyone loses precious awareness and integritylxv. This, in turn, has predisposed uncountable generations of individuals to adopt the contemporary paradigm as correct (including adopting the permanent war economy and violence as essential aspects of "our way of life").

Shame and the Diminution of the Sacred

"Attempting to live the sacred in modern civilization is often denigrated in a civilization where spirituality threatens the constructs of consensus reality agreements, and the 'business as usual' paradigm." lxvi For many, if not most people, shame was used as a weapon, a cudgel, to force, reinforce and manipulate behaviors that were considered desirable by parents and, by extension, other authority figures. Rather than providing a perceptual framework within which to make adjustments for behaviors, shame becomes an internalized mandate demanding attention in order to avoid negative consequences.

"A shame crisis may develop when the child's 'boundless exhibitionism' meets unexpected parental disapproval... [thereafter striving to] develop a concept of the desired self [that the parents require] ..." a template for future behavior and self-worth." lxvii Janoff-Bulmanlxviii pointed out that "Much of the psychological trauma produced by victimizing events derives from the shattering of very basic assumptions that victims have held about the operation of the world," this "rupture of trust in oneself is one's assessment of reality, one's simple sense of competence for being in the world. It is this disruption of connectedness that elicits the effect of shame." lxix

Shamed Desire

The term "cognitive dissonance" to refer to a condition in which one of a pair of cognitions follows from the converse of the other (e.g., smiling broadly and saying: "I'm very sad").

When one experiences "shamed desire,"lxx one perceives one's desire as pure (e.g., "I want this"), while simultaneously feeling that such a desire is unworthy or shameful (e.g., to the self, or self-image) —" I'm not allowed," or "I don't deserve this." It is therefore rejected. One is simultaneously filled with a desire for a person or an action that must be disowned, repulsed, or repudiated. One might hope for fulfillment of some sort from enacting such desires, but it will almost always be accompanied by a sense of shame or remorse—a kind of double-bind situation in which one is unable to derive pleasure and satisfaction no matter which direction one may choose.

One may feel simultaneously victimized and compelled to utilize one's compulsion. One may become inured of this and adopt a victimized stance. One might adopt this as a way of avoiding responsibility for having made the initial choice.lxxi Wolinsky described this as an "Intrapersonal (self-to-self) trance."lxxii The burden of shame-based memories creates a "black hole hunger"lxxiii for intimacy.

Self-Repudiation

Shaming children often comes to be seen as corrective while it is actually a reinforcement of unexamined constituted authority.

Blaming oneself may seem self-protective at first glance. One repudiates one's true needs and attempts to incorporate the traumatic affect, thus, seemingly becoming more completely whole by building barriers around this painful self-expression, in an attempt to preserve some measure of a vital relationship with the perpetrator.lxxiv

An extreme example is cutting, a self-mutilating behavior rooted in a deep shamed sense of self that that will respond to treatment that is both receptive and non-shaming. lxxv It embodies the paradoxical nature of meeting the family system's needs while simultaneously denying the child's needs. One may become one's own perpetrator, developing autohypnotic tendencieslxxvi to reinforce one's personal entrancement lxxvii to the perceived needs and opinions of others.

One may also make a vainglorious attempt to live in denial of one's tainted knowledge, pretending it does not exist—though the effects will continue to manifest (i.e., depression, phobias) or it may also surface as triggered affect, even a full-blown flashback.

Freud idealized his father (and the paternalistic society) as being proper and correct. He embraced the hypocritical and misogynistic ideals of his age in order to repudiate his shame, both in his personal life and his writings.lxxviii He disowned the palpable facts and abandoned what he then called "seduction theory"lxxix because, as he wrote "Then came the surprise at the fact that in every case the father, not excluding my own, had to be blamed as a pervert…such a widespread extent of perversity toward children is, after all, not probable."lxxx The Oedipus and Electra complexes, which blame sexual abuse on the fantasies of children, most likely developed also as a defense against his own shame about his abuse by his father.lxxxi

Delusion

Delusion is a "False belief maintained in the face of overwhelming evidence to the contrary." lxxxii There is a protective aspect to delusion. If, for example, one feels weak and helpless, yet manages to convince oneself that one is strong and powerful, (perhaps under the influence of substances), one might act as if one had great power (e.g., "I'm taking over Bill Graham's rock empire!"), and be confused, upset, or angry when the "world at large" fails to agree. The purest form of delusion is not substance induced and is likely created by an individual out of inner need and torment. This may often be fueled by the fear of psychological death—fear of annihilation, ergo, ceasing to exist. It is, in fact, the death of the earlier conceptions of self that gives rise to a succession of more mature, and hopefully more fully developed, images.

Codependence could be considered to be delusional, in the sense that shame leads one to shape one's behaviors to meet the perceived needs of the other, hoping that it might magically transform the other into someone who actually fulfills one's needs. An example of this would be a situation in which the sober partner carries the torch for the recovery of the alcoholic partner, believing he or she will then magically be transformed into the partner s/he always wanted.

Woundedness

We are all wounded. "The wound is the womb from which we are continually born…Giftedness and woundedness condition each other—they grow in relation to each other." Hence there is no escape from the wound, just continually developing a better understanding and integration of the material that is held in shadow or woundedness. "The gift awakens the wound… [and] Compassion arises out of woundedness." The gift is the higher octave of the wound. Immersion in the pain renders us incapable of recognizing the beauty and strength that lies in and behind our woundedness. In attempting to avoid or distract ourselves from our wound, we ignore or obviate the gift that always accompanies it. lxxxiii

The word pathology is derived from the Ancient Greek, and actually means "the study of passions."lxxxiv Only later (in transition through Old French) did it come to mean the "study of disease." Meade spoke eloquently to this when he defined depression and numbness as "A measure of our not hearing or being willing to hear the genius of the world…Great things are often hidden because one has to work hard to find them." The closer one gets to one's natural gifts, the more one encounter the wound. Impossible tasks may bring out one's best gifts in an attempt to breach the possibility. Consumer society requires that people 'forget' that they are wounded." In doing so, one ignores one's genuine inborn authority, in favor of positional authority that is granted by one's status in society and is usually abusive and corrupt.

CHAPTER FOUR
SHAME-BASED
CHILDREARING

All truth passes through three stages: First, it is ridiculed; second, it is violently opposed; third, it is accepted as self-evident.
Arthur Schopenhauer, (apocryphal).

Disrupted Development

If one identifies with being wounded, one may develop focus his or her entire life around it, perpetuating one's sense of deficiency and retarding one's healing. The presence of a "sympathetic witness, one who confirms the child's perceptions" may make it more likely that he or she recognizes the wrong and will "help the child experience his or her feelings to some degree." This may allow the child to "escape psychosis as well as total self-alienation (which characterizes the life of so many abused people)." lxxxv

It is highly possible that society itself may become a vector of transmission of shame. By embodying and promoting the dominant ethos as "normal," separatist societal influences promote as "normal" most "isms"—racism, sexism, homophobia, ageism, and classism, and embrace, indeed, rely upon permanent war to drive the economy. This simply continues the shame initiated in the childhood experiences of shame that disregard the beauty and sovereignty of all individuals

Shame and Codependence

Codependence has been defined as any "Relationship or partnership in which two or more people support or encourage each other's unhealthy habits." lxxxvi Attempting to live up to an ideal fostered by one's parents is a set up for failure and future addictive behaviors, as the child's adaptive efforts to please others in order to garner positive self-feeling is a "core component of a relationship addict."lxxxvii

The current global society is predatory—not only creating social conditions that marginalize individuals and groups but allowing them to be exploited. Thus, an individual matures encased in a container of pre-existing ideas and beliefs that form the basis for decision-making and influence that individual's personal naïve reality.

Very few individuals are encouraged to investigate the roots of their shame, usually choosing to simply escape it as quickly as possible. One adopts avoidance, having learned it as a survival tool. Happiness is the elusive, vapid, quicksilver experience that one elects to experience in order to momentarily "forget" one's pain.

One aspect of this is the continual re-creation of myth of the love of one's parents, no matter how much one has been shamed or abused. We are taught to "love, honor, and obey." They, in turn, inculcate in their children a blind obedience to all adults, to all other "authorities." They, as adults, actively support the fantasy of loving parents and of a benevolent society.

Children as Commodities

Corporatized society has come to include children as a commodity, perhaps the biggest, commodity on the planet. Many countries make an open fact of exploiting children for sexual and industrial uses—and the United States maintains "diplomatic relations" with them (e.g., India, Thailand, Philippines) as well as tolerating (despite official efforts to the contrary) a thriving child pornography industry.

Besides that, advertising is aimed at children; laws are enacted to proscribe children's behaviors and activities or mandate their being forcibly drugged (vaccinations and ADHD "treatments") by school authorities." Parents are mythologized as being devoted to their children, yet the incidents of abuse and torture of children escalate every year. Children are among the most exploited beings on the Earth. Every year, 3.3 million reports of child abuse are made in the United States alone, involving nearly 6 million children (any report may include multiple children). The United States has the worst record of any industrialized nation—losing four to seven children every day to abuse-related deaths. lxxxviii

The number of psychotropic drug prescriptions for children 2 years old and younger has jumped 50 percent from 2013 to 2014.lxxxix Over one million children under the age of five are prescribed and taking psychiatric medications.xc

The most usual source of exploitation is the parents themselves, many of whom create children to get their own incomplete emotional needs met as if through "ownership" of children. Again, as Miller has noted, "As children we have no history standing in our way, and our tolerance of our parents knows no bounds. The love a child has for his or her parents ensures that their conscious or unconscious acts of mental cruelty will go unnoticed.xci

If children are coerced or threatened to believe that they ought to not be angry, "selfish," show independence, and/or "willfulness" in the face of parental demands/mandates, a secondary shame may be induced when rage is suppressed—further isolating and alienating the child from the innate sense of well-being once known in the womb. A child may develop a shame-avoidant approach to living, or learn either to deny one's shame, or refuse to take responsibility, or both. In denial, one may choose to not think about or discuss the arenas in which, or about which, one feels ashamed—thus attempting to avoid them and thus, prevent their healing.

If, for example, one wishes to avoid shame about one's sexuality (for any of a number of reasons), one may attempt to avoid thinking about sex (except in a shamed manner); may avoid approaching potential partners who are otherwise appealing. Or one may be fearful or ashamed of: 1) feeling sexually aroused; 2) feeling

38

sexually drawn to potential partners; 3) feeling sexually attracted to particular potential partners; or 4) feeling that one must not allow one's sexual attraction to show, and thus believe that one must "manage" one's sexual energy in a less-than-visible manner (i.e., masturbating privately, or having assignations with prostitutes).

There are innumerable ways shame is passed on to, and absorbed by, the sponge-like developing brains of children, such as abandonment, severe emotional abuse, neglect, and/or violence). This may enmesh such an individual in the needs of the family system—doing what is required to survive, becoming the false self who meets the needs and/or mandates of others. It is ultimately a vain attempt to balance the discordant emotional needs or demands of others because the child's survival is intricately related to the relative stability of the family's structure. Important survival figures might have behaviors that cannot be predicted (or appeased). The child may suffer, even die, literally or metaphorically. At the least the child will become captive to the warped emotional mandates of others, a prisoner of childhood.

Some Political Considerations

Any individual will typically adopt a set of values like their culture and family of origin. As individuals mature, they begin to consciously assert their beliefs and values as "correct." One might even begin to take a certain amount of pride in specific values, and without necessarily questioning them.

Most people deny the exquisite sensitivity of children because they are in denial of their own lost legacy of sensitivity. Many who choose to deny their own tenderness fit in perfectly with the impersonal machine-oriented business ethic, the and embrace its emotionally and spiritually vacant tenets, are superbly rewarded because they support the existing power system—one that, in my estimation, recreates or recapitulates the shame-based childrearing system.

In a misguided effort to develop stability in a corporate system designed to obviate emotional and spiritual awareness, they are hailed as heroes and heroines. They are featured in newspapers and magazines. They are the saviors in popular books. Everyone is encouraged to aspire to be like them. Global media embraces and lionizes them. Yet the fact is that 95% of all media is owned by six multinational corporations,xcii reinforcing the economic and social imbalance as culturally sanctioned and just "the way it is." Human lives, human souls, are sacrificed daily in the ever-growing hunger for corporate profits, masked by the purported "need" for more of everything, especially war and its related requirements.

CHAPTER FIVE
TRAUMA

Much of the psychological trauma produced by victimizing events derives from the shattering of very basic assumptions that victims have held about the operation of the world.

Janoff-Bulman, 1985, p. 17.

The Biochemistry of Trauma

Trauma has been defined as "An abrupt physical disruption in ordinary life experience, often with loss of control over the body." xciii Trauma conditions the way in which one responds to future similar incidents—conditioning one to become more concerned, more tentative, or more reactive in altering the manner of one's response, and thereinafter altering the creation of one's "reality" in tune with one's history of traumatic experiences.

One's memories are never completely erased, though one may significantly alter one's pain or shame response. There are a vast number of physiological changes attributed to trauma: increases in heart rate, blood sugar, muscular tension, and perspiration; dilation of the pupils; and hyperventilation which may lead to irregular heart rate, dizziness, shortness of breath, choking sensations, lump in the throat, heartburn, chest pain, blurred vision, numbness or tingling of extremities, muscle pains or spasms, nausea, shaking, fatigue, and confusion or inability to concentrate. xciv

Rossixcv and van der Kolkxcvi reported that the symptoms of psychic numbing, and the related hyper-alert states of Posttraumatic Stress Disorder (PTSD) may be related to neurotransmitter depletions.

Matsakisxcvii noted that depletion of major neurotransmitters secondary to stress are "Norepinephrine (noradrenaline), dopamine, serotonin, endogenous opioids, and catecholamines." Adrenaline precipitates an exaggerated response, while norepinephrine initiates an under-reactive response. Since these directly modulate the intensity of emotion, the amplification or depletion of these can lead to erratic emotional responses or mood swings. Indeed, artificially lowering the levels of these neurotransmitters in animals has been shown to trigger an "emergency response."

"Biological shifts also have been found to create difficulties in four other areas: thinking clearly, regulating the intensity of emotions, relating to other people, and sustaining hope for the future." xcviii Trauma also has also been shown to have an effect on three other important psychological functions: the ability to modulate strong feelings, associated with self-soothing; the ability to maintain emotional connections with others; and the ability to maintain a positive self-identity.xcix The net result of these combined losses often lends themselves to an individual becoming marginalized, isolated, and withdrawn.

Traumatic Bonding

Traumatic bonding occurs as "Anxiously intensified attachment behavior," as a result of "Chronic victimization in an emotionally powerful relationship."c Traumatic memories are "Often encoded in procedural repertoires and somatosensory modalities, rather than declarative, explicit memory."ci Addictions may develop as an adaptive process that initially may seem to lessen the felt-severity of the trance and add an incredibly tangled web of complications.

Traumatic amnesia is an unusual, but frequently reported phenomenon, wherein one becomes amnesic for certain details or portions of a terrifying event, cii especially if the memory disruptions are so terrifying that the normal biological processes underlying information storage are disrupted.

Triggers

Any aspect of a traumatic experience may be abruptly and vividly: sights, sounds, tastes, smells, textures, people, situations and/or environments related to the original trauma. This process of triggering is related to the more deeply the traumatic material has affected one. The more profound one's dissociation, the greater the potential for an exaggerated response in the present (e.g., heightened startle response; bursts of rage; or even wanting to put a bullet through an engine block when a car alarm activates). Any of these triggers may become the proximal cause of a re-awakened memory and reaction, as if the original traumatic incident and/or affect were being repeated in the present. An individual who has been chronically traumatized may become inured of such memory retrieval, and thus attract other such situations. For example, a traumatized individual may actually remain in an abusive environment, or with an abusive person because he or she has become accustomed to the trauma.ciii

Flashbacks

The homeostatic process constantly works to balance any previously unintegrated experience, allowing greater relative freedom of and for an individual's energies. civ A flashback is simply "The recurrence of a memory or reliving an experience from the past." cv Flashbacks may be an attempt to fully remember and work through "stuck" dissociative stances.cvi The more vivid the sensory prompt, the more the likelihood of its being recalled (i.e., red more than white; sweet more than sour). Flashbacks may represent an aspect of uncontrolled autohypnosis... immersion into a powerful positive hallucinatory state so profound that all other immediate perceptions are dissociated, and the individual temporarily loses the capacity to distinguish memory from current experience. cvii Any trigger may set off a flashback, that may represent: (a) an attempt to ward off the current danger; (b) heal the original trauma-induced (and unresolved) deficit through more complete recall; (c) signal a retreat to an earlier emotional age at which one (mistakenly) believes one may have felt safer, or (d) or an aberrant attempt to self-soothe a regressed state.

For example, if one has suppressed rage, it may surface in a situation that may seem inappropriate. Expressing rage neither heals nor eliminates its self-protective force, as it may express itself anytime a tender area is touched. Rage is timeless. It is a shame-avoidant technique that an individual may adopt to not feel diminished. It will remain active in one's emotional vocabulary until it is healed. The reaction may actually seem age-inappropriate at first glance since the original injury lies in the earliest years. Rage is always a sign of deep injury being triggered with tremendous affect, seeking to voice often deeply buried material.

There are safe ways to heal rage (e.g., Primal Therapy; Gestalt; Voice Dialogue; Shadow Work), though these really require the guidance of a professional. By experiencing the source of one's emotions and safely expressing them, one may indeed change one's life in potentially profound ways. Research indicates that the brain may suffer pernicious effects from abuse that actually "mediate development in vulnerable brain regions" as follows:

Limbic irritability. This is manifested by markedly increased prevalence of symptoms suggestive of temporal lobe epilepsy, and by an increased incidence of clinically significant EEG (brain wave) abnormalities. [This indicates the possibility of sensory, motor, perceptual, and/or emotional changes].

Deficient development and differentiation of the left hemisphere. This may manifest throughout the cerebral cortex and the hippocampus. [This may include heightened right hemispheric development, and a deficiency in development of the left— impairing language development, verbal memory, and inducing dissociative symptoms].

Deficient left-right hemisphere integration. This indicates marked shifts in hemispheric activity during memory recall, and by underdevelopment of the middle portions of the corpus callosum, the primary pathway connecting the two hemispheres.

Abnormal activity in the cerebellar vermis (the middle strip between the two hemispheres of the brain). This appears to play an important role in emotional and attentional balance and regulates electrical activity within the limbic system. [This may indicate decreased serotonin production in the hippocampus, decreased receptors for glucocorticoids leading to increased sensitivity to fear, and a heightened adrenaline response. There may also be suppressed immune and inflammatory responses]. cviii

CHAPTER SIX
DISSOCIATION

Dissociation is perhaps the most common characteristic of the human condition. Many of us are dissociated from our bodies, from our feelings, from some of our actions and from many of our memories.

Springer, 1994, p. v.

Definition

Dissociation is defined as "A disruption in the usually integrated functions of consciousness, memory, identity, or perception of the environment."cix Any of an individual's ordinarily accessible perceptions, memories, and emotions may be affected by this interference that, over time, may become rooted as a primary way of reacting to stress, threat or danger.

One may act as if:

As if a piece of the external world, which is now within the person but is not part of that person, constitutes a continuing focus of stress acting from within. This internalized stressor now exists outside of time, in an unstable state, and, unless and until it is fully experienced, it will continue to exert its effect indefinitely. cx

Etiology

In the Nineteenth Century, Janet first recognized dissociation as appearing in traumatized individuals unconsciously attempting to exclude memories of sexual abuse from consciousness.cxi Van der Kolk described dissociation as occurring when the state of physical hyperarousal experienced in a traumatic situation is so intense that one's ability to reason and remember decreases radically, and the brain cannot comprehend, or otherwise make sense of the experience (cognitive shock). These memories are then split off from conscious awareness, and either stored as fragments, or on a less than conscious level.cxii Phenomena such as emotional numbing, psychogenic amnesia, and flashbacks may represent an "Incomplete or partial experiencing of the traumatic material in the body/mind system."cxiii

One may become so inured of trauma and of responding to it by dissociating, one might begin to believe that trauma is a "natural" state, to the point where one might unconsciously invite traumatic situations,cxiv even to the point wherein it might become one's normal method of coping, even in situation wherein the level of trauma is less than overwhelming.cxv This may, in turn, further "undermine the very sense of self that seeks vitality from adaptation. The decline in autonomy is accompanied by a loss of genuine agency, of the self's capacity to mobilize inner power, act effectively, and initiate constructive behavior."cxvi A dissociative episode may: 1) ward off the current danger; 2) be an attempt to heal the original traumatogenic deficit (by withdrawing to allow healing); 3) allow one to retreat to an earlier emotional age at which one (mistakenly) believes one may have felt safer; and/or 4) allow one to attempt to self-soothe the regressed child state.

Dissociation and the False Self

Shame-based childrearing lends itself to some form of dissociation in everyone (via coercion, and a sense of power differential), which may be the reason it seems common to the entire human population.cxvii One may experience dissociation from one's body, feelings, actions and/or memories. One may be led to be normatively dissociative to meet the demands of culture, and this facilitates the creation of the false self. cxviii

Individuals who are not toxically shamed during the earliest years may certainly be traumatized later in life, but the impact will be less broad and intense, as a firmer foundation exists upon which one's identity lies. The traumatic experiences may potentially strengthen the personality by making it stronger and more resilient cxix, while the beneficial psychological effects of dissociation acting as a psychic shield. cxx

Projection

Projection is a psychic mechanism in which "Intolerable feelings, impulses, or thoughts are falsely attributed to other people." cxxi An individual may be so filled with self-denying shame that he or she may externalize the inner need for emotional satisfaction, creating a seemingly insatiable hunger to be filled (e.g., food and compulsive eating). In this instance, one literally externalizes this unmet need by consuming more than is needed for satiety, seeking to fill the inner with the outer. Thus, the excess weight gained and retained, and the continued cravings for food, may reflect not only the hunger for fulfillment, but also either the failure to let go of the emotional weight of previous traumatic memories, or an attempt to avoid feeling their significance.

Projection may present more seriously, when the intensity of rage is so powerful that one believes that others are opposed or threatening one. This distorted belief then allows one to maintain a negative self-image and attitude that justifies defensiveness, even violence toward others. One may not have any sense of either feeling the rage or being personally accountable for it (after all, it is the other's fault!), that temporarily allows one to escape having to deal with emotionally intolerable feelings. (This is the stereotypic violence of the schizophrenic that is so touted by the media).

When children fail or are not allowed, to express their true feelings of shock and outrage at insensitive, shameful, or abusive treatment, they may assume an inverse parental role, pretending to be more "acceptably" mature; or may adopt the wounded child aspect—allowing the shame-wounded adult to project his or her emotional needs onto the child with seeming impunity. This may grant momentary relief to the adult, believing that he or she has effectively blamed the child for whatever fault has incurred the wrath of the perpetrator (e.g., "See what you made me do," or "The child seduced me").

Since any projection allows for a momentary respite from the unrelenting pressures of shame, one may become addicted to this process. In this way, all addictions may become shame-avoidant, with the object of the obsession momentarily displacing the disallowed or unobtainable internalized awareness.

This may also be a factor in suicide. When one internalizes the projections of the perpetrator, this material may continue to contaminate one's consciousness. Further, if one assumes that the introjected material is real, and is one's own genuine feeling, there is the strong possibility of identifying with both the feeling and the resulting shame. If one then sincerely desires to disown the internalized shame of the perpetrator, the idea of suicide ideation may come to the fore as an attempt to do so—in effect, killing the "bad" inside of me by killing my body. Traumatized individuals "are at one and the same time themselves and the oppressor whose consciousness they have internalized."cxxii

Bradshaw described "Turning against the Self:"

The extreme form of this is suicidality. In such cases (the French call it self-murder), the person so identifies with the offender that he is killing the offender by killing himself. Common, but less intense examples include nail-biting, head-banging, accident-proneness and self-mutilation. In later life, people may injure themselves socially or financially.cxxiii

Multiplicity or Multidimensionality?

Talbot referred to "the holographic universe," cxxiv and its innate multidimensionality, yet mainstream psychology is essentially concerned with pathology and exclusiveness, and generally ignores, or is even hostile toward, realms of relatedness and experience that are not within the purview of the immediate senses. This approach, however, ignores the fact that each of us lives in multiple domains simultaneously (i.e., physical, emotional, psychological, mental, spiritual). This truncated approach retards personal growth since

The systems' approach indicates that latent human potential can be developed and used in various discreet altered states, so that learning to shift into the discreet altered state appropriate for dealing with a problem is part of psychological growth. cxxv

Springer stated that "awareness can extend into higher and higher (or deeper and deeper) levels of consciousness and provide the container for a tremendous amount of multiplicity...The more deeply aware I am, the more I can embrace my own multiplicity, and the similar multiplicity of others." cxxvi

Stone and Stonecxxvii formulated a therapeutic approach that utilizes giving voice to "subpersonalities," referring to one's unexpressed personality aspects as having separate existences.

Some research has suggested that dissociation can be healthy, with the key lying "in the areas of awareness, associative access, and choice"; and that it is "unconscious, unchoice, habitual, or 'stuck' dissociation that is problematic, not dissociation per se."cxxviii It is possible that "the phenomenon of dissociation into more than one personality, each with a separate sense of self-identity, allows for complex transformative processes to occur within the 'community of selves.'" cxxix

Rosscxxx spoke of the possibility of there being a Cultural dissociation barrier...to keep other part-selves suppressed, out of contact and communication with the executive self, and relegated to second class status in the mind... to include the receiver/transmitter for extrasensory and paranormal experiences, programs responsible for running the physical body, and the deep intuitive consciousness.

CHAPTER SEVEN
ADDICTIONS PART I

Blocked energy flow makes pools of negative emotion, which generate character flaws. All character flaws can be boiled down to one statement: addicts do not know how to take care of themselves

Herlong & Herlong, 1995, p. 148.

Definition

The word addiction is derived from "addictus," (L., "given over").cxxxi It has been defined as "An obsessive dependency on people, substances, money, material goods, or situations," lcxxxii or "Any pathological relationship with any mood-altering experience that has life-damaging consequences." cxxxiii

The idea of addiction as disease developed out of the moralistic and racist rhetoric of the temperance and anti-opium movements of the nineteenth century, linking addiction to drugs and illness and suggesting that it was a medical problem was used to scare people away from drugs.

There was a fallacy in that thinking that was completely missed or purposefully overlooked. When we consider whether drug addiction is a disease, we are concerned with what causes the drug to get into the body. It's quite irrelevant what the drug does after it's in the body. This uncontroversial fact is quite distinct from any claim that the activity itself is a disease ...A simple test of a true physical disease is whether it can be shown to exist in a corpse...No such identifiable pathology has been found in the bodies of heavy drinkers and drug addicts. This alone justifies the view that addiction is not a physical disease." cxxxiv

Another innate human trait, novelty seeking—free-fall parachute jumping, car racing and other high-thrill behaviors—was erroneously left out of the equation, especially since such activities have a deep and intimate correlation with addictions since both types of activities stimulate the mesolimbic dopamine reward pathway, which has evolved because it "sub serves behaviors that are vital to survival." cxxxv

"If novelty seeking and drug seeking involve a similar brain system, then novel stimuli might substitute for drug reward...Behaviors that stimulate the mesolimbic dopamine reward system may be most useful in substituting for drug rewards."

Etiology

Addiction has probably been around as long as humanity. According to the King County Bar Project (KCBP)cxxxvi, there may be an evolutionary basis for substance use. Coffee, tea, tobacco, and cocoa were always regulated, and prohibited, by European Empire-builders because they were imported from "savage lands." It was more driven by the clashing of cultures and the defenders of the home turf than by any inherent qualities or properties of the substances themselves.

Consumption of coffee and tobacco were even punishable by death in certain parts of Europe and the Middle East until the 17th century. England and France fought the Opium Wars during the nineteenth century in order to secure dominion over what was then the $5 Billion (equivalent of almost $100 Billion today) per annum drug trade.cxxxvii

The liberation may be fleeting, but the function of addiction is always to neurologically disinhibit one's brain. All addictions are shame-avoidant, and create dissociated states evoked by traumatic experiences. This may be so even if the drugs are culturally and legally approved.

Heroin was refined from morphine base by Bayer in 1898, ostensibly as a better analgesic. Bayer sent out 100,000 free samples to doctors along with samples of aspirin (created in 1899). Cocaine was an original ingredient in Coca-Cola, and other popular nostrums, and was patented by Parke-Davis in the early 1890s. (Sigmund Freud was actually well-paid to advertise its "exhilarating" effects, while at the same time the U.S. Surgeon General endorsed cocaine's use for medical purposes). Taxes on psychoactive substances provided a significant part of government revenue for modern nations prior to the advent of income taxation.

"The very act of explaining drug abuse in certain habitual ways might help to maintain and develop drug problems in those terms," cxxxviii while Peele noted that "the regular pursuit by many of an eradication of awareness is an expression of mainstream cultural trends." cxxxix

Medical Model

Addicts seek an addictive experience to achieve a desired feeling...[that] is powerful, gratifying, and ultimately becomes both necessary and distressing...while perceiving this excess to signal a lack of control that defines addiction for themselves and others. cxl

The medicalization of emotional and moral problems has given greater impetus to the medical model. "When it was formally endorsed by the American Medical Association in 1956, the disease model was given biomedical legitimacy."cxli The use of the word "addiction" in this model refers to loss of control, withdrawal, and tolerance.

The medical model posits that physical agents cause diseases; and that neutralizing the physical agent will heal the disease (e.g., treating an infection with penicillin). Many researchers and clinicians have addressed the distorted notion of applying medical model to a mental-emotional phenomenon.

The tenets of the disease model are predicated on a model that incorporates a lack of responsibility and autonomy.

1) Most addicts don't know they have a problem and must be

forced to recognize that they are addicts.

2) Addicts cannot control themselves when they take drugs.

3) The only solution to addiction is treatment.

4) Addiction is an all-or-nothing disease: A person cannot be a temporary addict with a mild addiction.

5) The most important step in overcoming addiction is to acknowledge that you are powerless and can't control it.

6) Complete abstinence, not moderation, is the only way to control addiction.

7) Physiology alone, not psychology, determines whether one person will become addicted and another will not.

8) The fact that addiction runs in families means that it is a genetic disease.

9) People who are addicted can never outgrow addiction and are always in danger of relapsing. cxlii

Brief Critique of the Medical Model

"Addictions usually occur within a social system that colludes by denying the problem," cxliii while Schaler noted, "Viewing people as if they are things that are caused, justifies paternalism," and allows for "Legal policies where adults are regarded by powerful others as if they were children incapable of being responsible for their own behaviors." cxliv

Addicted culture defines the limits of normalcy and pathology according to skewed standards called "Pathomorphic distortion, the idea that we define our standards of normalcy from trying to understand and treat illness." cxlv

Free Will Model

Juxtaposed to the mandates of the disease model is the free-will model, grounded in the notion of individual self-efficacy—the idea that one has the confidence in one's own ability to achieve a specific goal in a specific situation. The tenets of this model postulate:

1) The best way to overcome addiction is to rely on your own will power (you are your 'higher power').

2) People can stop depending on addictions as they develop other ways to deal with life.

3) Addiction has more to do with the environment people live in than the substance or process to which they are addicted.

4) People often outgrow addictions.

5) Addicts can learn to moderate their addictions.

6) People become addicted when life is going badly for them.

7) Addicts can and often do find their own ways out of addictions, without outside help.

8) You have to rely on yourself to overcome addiction.

9) Addiction is often a way of life upon which people rely to

cope, or avoid coping, with the world (adapted from Schaler cxlvi).

Individuals have interpersonal relationship problems prior to drug use, and "Use drugs and get into negative addictions because they kid themselves that they can somehow solve problems by deadening themselves to those problems"; and "A person suffering from a harmful addiction…actually has a different problem not obviously related to the addiction." Peelecxlvii commented that "The key to addiction, seen in this light, is its persistence in the face of harmful consequences for the individual." cxlviii

Addicts direct their powerful will to assure themselves a ready supply of their addiction of choice, though. We often tend to applaud those who ruthlessly subordinate their lives to an over-riding purpose we consider valuable; we often tend to boo and hiss those who ruthlessly subordinate their lives to an over-riding purpose we consider pointless or destructive. Considered in this way, addiction becomes an ethical issue. cxlix

Addiction as Delusion

Substance abuse is delusional in the sense that one uses addictive substances or experiences to buffer or alter one's own inner deficiencies—especially viewing them in a positive light when they have deleterious effects on one's body and relationships. The transitory effects become the justification for the belief that one may magically avoid the consequences of one's actions. (This could easily qualify as "grandiose"). And one might then perceive the

60

ensuing crash or come down as "persecutory" (when one falls back into a pre-existing depressed or chaotic mood).

One may be driven to use food or sex or heroin to drive away shame; to create the illusion of self-value, or adequacy; to create a sense of pseudo-functionality; or to blank out the unrelenting awareness of one's emotional poverty. All of this may be done to seek a kind of personal redemption (Latin, "to buy back").

Addiction and Dissociation

One may become inured of their own hormones and neurotransmitters. In this sense, addiction is autohypnotic. One may become addicted to his or her own body chemistry,cl most notably to adrenalinecli In a similar manner, this may also relate to the autohypnotic nature of the addiction process.clii

Tolerance leads inevitably to an increasing demand in order to maintain this "hedonic tone,"cliii and may become an obsessive pursuit. It may even become a raison d'être, as Reedcliv once said of heroin, "It's my life, it's my wife…when I rush and, on the run, I feel just like Jesus' son." The drug may be the "magic carpet" that allows momentary relief from the otherwise intractable emotional pain. The choice of addiction may be encouraged or "authorized" by one's role modeling figures and/or the larger society.

CHAPTER EIGHT
ADDICTIONS PART II

When mothering persons have been deprived of their own healthy narcissism, they will try to get it for the rest of their lives through a substitute means. The most available object for narcissistically deprived parents is their own children

Miller, 1990, p. 4.

"Authorizing" Addictions

Addictions may be "authorized" through role-modeling by one's family and/or society at large, in certain culturally "approved" ways. Parents who use legal or illegal substances, and/or practices such as excessive rage or masturbation, to attempt to "fix" their anxiety, depression, or anger. They create a living example for their children that may create cravings secondary to the traumatic bond created with significant figures in childhood.

Coffee or tobacco, or practices such as gambling, are declared "legal," while others (like marijuana) are forbidden. A child might choose to smoke cigarettes to stanch his anxiety, mirroring the role modeling of the parents. Jungclv observed that children carry the burden of the unlived lives of their parents.

I experienced one example of cultural authorization when I was in Taiwan (Republic of China) in 1969. One could easily and openly buy opium, morphine, or heroin. The dominant society considered it to be traditional. In responding to cultural and economic pressures, the government had enacted extremely stringent laws against marijuana in an attempt to keep out the "influence of the Western devils."

A five-year sentence was justified for the first offense, ten years for the second, while life in prison without the possibility of parole was the unhappy lot of a three-time offender.

An example of familial authorization occurred while I was working at the Mount Zion Hospital Crisis Clinic in San Francisco. I interviewed this young client who had been drunk in public and was brought in by the police for "acting crazy." After he sobered up, it was clear that he had only been drunk, not psychotic. Since he was a minor, I had to call an adult family member to pick him up. He refused but was unwilling to tell me why. Finally, he told one of the social workers that he was afraid to go home because his mother, her boyfriend, and an aunt were all heroin addicts. Then he further told us that his grandmother (who owned the house where he lived) considered herself to be a strict Christian, and would beat him for having gotten drunk, though she considered the heroin abuse acceptable!

A Plug for Drugs

I want to address a deeper level of research, informed by my own personal experiences as a "living laboratory" for altered states for many years. I believe that there are three distinct stages or phases of substance abuse and dependence that I will shortly delineate.

Substance abuse is "The maladaptive use of a drug resulting in impairment or distress," clvi resulting in any number of social and emotional dysfunctions. Most definitions of substance abuse tend to be pejorative, prejudiced in favor of the so-called mainstream society, viewing it as pathological.

We live in an addicted society that influences activities within multiple spheres for profit. Viewed through this lens, one might see the media-related propaganda on "The War on Drugs" as a smokescreen to create and reinforce authoritarian attitudes. One could see substance dependence, and especially recovery, as having the potential to be aspects of a spiritual and emotional transformation, especially if it is divorced from every aspect of commodified modern life.

Suppression of Altered States

The tight, even draconian, suppression of most substances that induce altered states, has led to their being either banned or made illegal. Neither is one generally allowed, under the current glut of repressive laws, to heal oneself through any means other than those approved by the medical model—essentially the rampant consumerist-approved trillion-dollar prescription drug industry.

Law and government have always been two of the primary vectors through which individuals have been suppressed, though the desire for mood alteration has always occurred throughout humanity's history. Even insects seek altered states, like leaf cutter ants who capture and cultivate Platyrhopalopsis melyi, a small beetle that the ants stimulate by stroking its belly to secrete a sweet potion that is intoxicating, perhaps even psychedelic, for them.clvii

The criminalization of many sacred substances that induce altered states and may lead to alternate life choices that are in opposition to the ruling regime, have always been affected (e.g., the death penalty for possessing tobacco or cocoa until the 17th Century in Europe). The Twelfth through Sixteenth Centuries marked an increase in the suppression of autonomy-embracing activities and especially altered states by the governments and the Catholic Church (e.g., the Inquisitions). This is especially evident in the highly institutionalized methods of healing approved by the patriarchyclviii paralleling our "Lost ability to enter into nature-induced non-ordinary states of consciousness for the purposes of healing, revelation, and connectedness.

"clix

In this context then, it's no real surprise then that alcohol and tobacco—two of the deadliest poisons known to man—are condoned, taxed, and freely allowed distribution, while psychedelic substances such as marijuana, LSD, and psilocybin are banned as "dangerous drugs" —despite the fact that they have great potential to be mind- and spirit-healing potential. This is, in large part, why they have been declared "illegal." This has intense political overtones in a fascist, repressive culture that works assiduously to maintain its hegemony, especially meting out punishments for using those substances that do not accord with the current political, pseudo-moral bent.

The United States has only five percent of the world's population, and yet has more people in prison than the entire rest of the planet (sixty percent of them for minor drug charges).clx Incarcerated Blacks outnumber Whites 7:1. The US also accounts for almost thirty eight percent of the world's cocaine consumption.clxiIn 1980, the prison population was 220 per 100,000; and had gone up 300% by 2010. For-profit prisons is the fastest growing industry in the U.S. They were 6% of prisons in 2004; 8.3% in 2008; and 35% in 2014. And the children of incarcerated people are 9 times more likely to become incarcerated.

Excessive alcohol use is the leading cause of preventable death, accounting for approximately 88,000 deaths per year from 2006–2010 and accounting for 1 in 10 deaths among working-age adults aged 20–64 years. Nearly 104 million Americans age 12 and older were using illegal drugs in the previous year—almost 38 percent of the population.clxii Drugs and alcohol cost taxpayers more than $143 billion annually in preventable health care costs, extra law enforcement, auto crashes, crime, and lost productivity.clxiii

War on Drugs, or War against People?

Living in an addictive society is extremely stressful and given the longstanding history of substance use and abuse, it is no small wonder that more and more citizens seek release via substances. Even after the psychedelic blowout of the 1960s; the cocaine- and heroin-drenched 1970s; the ecstasy and "club drugs" of the 1980s; methamphetamine in the 1990s and 2000s; the government chooses to pursue the failed strategy of the "War on Drugs," throwing astronomically unknown amounts of money at the elusive demons of substance abuse. One must seriously question the utter boondoggle this has become; and who is profiting from it in a very likely massive manner. No amount of pseudo-moralistic rhetoric will ever change the nature of the unmet needs of those who become pathological when they no longer have access to inner resources of healing.

When looked at more closely against the backdrop of the machinations of the corporate state, "The War against Drugs" is actually a war against people. The government is creating a quasi-therapeutic state in which the suppression of "illegal" substances has become a gigantic industry that is generating huge profits from many ancillary businesses, such as treatment, recovery, and prisons.

An example of such suppression is the "anti-smoking bigots" who are themselves addicted:

To the notion that the police should chase people who live

incorrectly, forcing them to comply with the currently fashionable definition of a wholesome lifestyle. The same goes for all those who wage a war on people, calling it a 'war on drugs.' clxiv

Cradle to grave profit! What better "business" for the profit-oriented Corporate State to be in than one in which one compels its citizens to "willingly" consume whatever product they are hooked on; to never question the origin of the addiction itself; and actually, pay money in order to maintain it, and eventually recover from it?

This is the "perfect plan," a meticulous disinformation scheme executed by the US Government, and its incestuous ties to large corporations, banks, agrobusiness combines, and the pharmaceutical companies. The bailout of the savings and loans in the 1980s, and the bailout of the major banks in the 2000's are just typical examples of the horrendous manipulation through disinformation that have led most people to simply stand still and be raped repeatedly while being told that it is for their "own good."

Any proposed mode of treating only the effects of drugs, not the underlying causes, is doomed to failure. It will not reach deeply enough into an individual's essential beingness, especially when viewed through the lens of contemporary medical (or disease) model—though this model is entirely aligned with the profit-making activities of capitalistic society (as I will explore in forthcoming chapters).

It will not work without overhauling the entire orientation of dualistic thinking and governance.

No amount of cogitation or intellectual discourse will ever effect a lasting change. Understanding addiction intellectually may only make it more frustrating if one believes one may (delusionally) think one's way out of it. Erecting a cognitive framework for what one has already experienced and begun to integrate is best done properly long after one has successfully stopped using.

A Small Personal Story

I have experienced many extreme states. One very vivid one occurred when I quit my $1000 a day cocaine habit in 1982 (after being strung out since 1979). I had progressed from snorting to free-basing and finally to injecting. I had long ago quit caring about clothing, cleanliness, food, or sex. I quit only when I had completely blown all of my resources, including my three connections (to all of whom I owed money). I was broke, way overdue with the rent (which I did not have); gas and electricity were turned off for lack of payment—and I had totally alienated everyone I had ever known. Yet the only thing I could think about was cocaine. The only thing I wanted was cocaine. The only thing I needed was cocaine.

This was the end after three years of sleeping for twenty-four hours every fifth day, and then getting up and doing it all again. When all of the struts and supports of my world disintegrated, I honestly do not remember how many days and nights I slept. It seemed at the time that it was about two months of sleeping and delirium for sixteen to eighteen hours every day. Most of the rest of the time was spent in bed crying, reading and immersed in castigating myself for the mess I had made of my life. Whatever else I might have done is lost to the fog of long-ago memory, though I remember that it was all related to cocaine craving and scheming— none of which had any effect. (I was also dodging two different people who were wanting to cause me great bodily harm for money owed for what had been fronted to me [provided "up front" with no down payment].

I was dazed and confused for many weeks at the very least. When I finally surfaced from the extreme lethargy, I was intensely craving cocaine. I had people looking to collect old debts watching my apartment building. I had totally ruined my reputation as a stand-up dope dealer, no one would even give me a single line.

In the aftermath of one of my delirious sleep-and-dream sessions, I was crying, shaking, totally depressed, completely exhausted. I threw my hands in the air and said, "Fuck it! I need some coke!"

As I stumbled around, filled with immense despair, a woman's voice spoke to me out of the corner of the ceiling. I wanted to believe I was just hallucinating, but I knew instantly that it was the voice of Divine Mother—who had come to me in several extreme situations since 1970. Her voice cut through my fog, but all I wanted was cocaine!

SHE said: "If you use again, you are going to die!"

I shook my head and went back to sleep as if in a coma. Some uncountable time later, I awoke remembering THE VOICE, but all I could think about was scoring—though with no money and no resources, I had no idea how.

Then, SHE spoke again from the corner of the room.

"If you use again, you are going to die!"

I really didn't give a damn if I lived or died. I wanted some cocaine!

THE VOICE had penetrated my emotional armor and I sat down on the end of the bed and sobbed.

I felt as if someone had taken a giant cleaver and slashed open my chest and laid it bare. I couldn't contain the flood that erupted from me. Between snatching breaths pseudo-asthmatically, I reviewed my life, begging for forgiveness, asking for release from this life. The heavy eruptions came wave after wave. Every time I believed they were over, some vagrant thought or feeling would trigger yet another torrent. I was hacking and spewing tremendous rivers of old toxins and corruption. I felt as if I had suffered a traumatic brain injury. I tore an intercostal muscle before I just tumbled to the floor, feeling like I might be taking my last breath filled with purple stars against a black field.

Later, when I could breathe again, I got to my feet, and threw my hands in the air, screaming, crying, begging.

"Please help me!"

I felt an immediate flood of soothing syrup saturate my tortured body, and my taste for cocaine was forever removed.

Along with extreme gratitude, I had only one thought: I want to live! I want to live! I want to live!

Aftermath

I am not trying to paint this experience as one even approaching enlightenment, or anything close. As the years have gone by, and my memory of that time has necessarily dimmed in vividness and acuity, I know only that from that starkly rendered moment on, I felt a release from my former life, a newfound strength and energy to go forward to do whatever I had to do to clean up my life and live in a better way. I was (at least momentarily) surrendered to the Divine forces of the Universe.

I knew, absolutely knew, I would be guided to whatever I had to do next—even though this was not the end of my travail. I have always been a very stubborn man. But in that moment, and in the subsequent weeks, I managed to keep a very small spark of hope alive in my chest, much like sheltering a last lit match in a monsoon wind.

In this sense, I say that extreme experiences may give birth to spiritual awakening. It does not matter one bit that mine came as a result of craving drugs; or that I would later fall into an environmental trap, and weaken, one brief moment, a single line, before finally relinquishing my cocaine habit forever on Christmas Eve 1982, in Sausalito.

The point is that I was caught in my free fall by divine forces that I believe are always there, if an individual reaches the utter end of whatever moorings he or she might have had, and is irrevocably cut loose from whatever one might have believed were personal possessions of thought and emotions—and, flailing helplessly, only to discover that there is far more to the Universe than meets the casual eye and ear of superficial beliefs when someone, something, answers a genuine cry for help in that moment of the utmost despair and fear.

CHAPTER NINE
SCARCITY AND SOCIAL
DARWINISM

---

*The road of excess leads to the palace of wisdom… You never know
what is enough, until you know what is more than enough*

Blake, 1790-93/1906

Enough

Greed is the most intense and virulent of addictions. It is the "norm" or lingua franca in Western societies. That, "naturally one should be greedy!" is an assumption feeds and is fed by, two closely related phenomena: the concept of enough and the productivity illusion.

In some sense, it does not matter how much of anything one has. It will never be enough since everyone seeks a state of inner fullness that masquerades as having enough of all manner of thoughts, feelings, expressions, substances, et cetera, in order to reach satiety. What lies at the root of this is the commonly held and accepted delusion we are all separate being; that there is no real connection between each of us and the Universe as a whole in the grand cosmic scheme; and that therefore, we must each constantly struggle and compete for scarce resources of every sort. In this sense, there never will be, or can be, enough.

The net effect of this illusion is that each of us endorses the notion that we must constantly work to produce more, in order to fulfill these delusional "needs" created by the loss of autonomy generated by the socialization process. Krishnamurti noted that "it is no measure of health to be well adjusted to a profoundly sick society."

Belief and "Reality"

We have been purposely misled, manipulated, and lied to for centuries, perhaps millennia. The muscular forces of commerce have always driven so called human progress to some extent, and it seems that there have always been oligarchs and plutocrats ruling the roost.

It is impossible to read even the most abridged versions of history without being aware of the great military campaigns waged by the lionized heroes of antiquity, many of whom were historically recorded as brutal and violent, especially toward conquered peoples. There is a thread that runs through them to contemporary times, though the ruthless conquerors of these so-called modern times wear $5000 grey pin-striped suits instead of armor and wield Meisterstück Mont Blanc pens instead of swords.

Greed and avarice are more nakedly displayed these days, and the populace is far more easily cowed into believing in and accepting their fate. It has not yet (so far at least) gotten to the point where individuals are arrested or slaughtered on the street for speaking against the government. It started slowly in Nazi Germany, and in Czarist Russia before the totalitarian state of the old Soviet Union. There is a growing fascism in the USA, intimately related to the usurpation of Constitutional guarantees and the abrogation of the Bill of Rights.

In fact, Roszakclxv spoke eloquently of this in his seminal book The Making of a Counterculture, one aspect of which was his deconstruction of the governmental styles of both the USA and the Soviet Union. One of his primary conclusions was that both systems are technocracies. The USSR used active force and violence to achieve its goals of social control, whereas the USA uses advertising and media-coercion to make it appear as if individuals were choosing to cooperate with social control. (Of course, this is backed by an incredible web of "law enforcement" and other "alphabeted" agencies used to enforce policies). Most people believe that they need Big Business and all of its component parts in order to survive, that such institutions are "normal," even "natural."

It is all in service of The Big Lie: "We must work for a living." It has promoted the myths that net worth equals self-worth; and that the government is actually "Of the people, by the people, and for the people"; and that corporations are beneficial and beneficent; and that the rest of us should be content to be serfs in thrall to their nobility. The net effect is to force the workers, the real producers, to live on the crumbs from their gold-plated tables. There is an almost endless list of people who have been murdered, tortured, assaulted, or socially marginalized for having the audacity to speak out against, or oppose, the blatant fascism that contradicts the idea of an equalitarian humanity. This titanic arrogance is upheld by the belief that those in power have been granted the "God-given" right to rule over others, that parades under the banner of Social Darwinism.

Social Darwinism

Part of the difficulty in establishing sensible and consistent usage is that commitment to the biology of natural selection and to "survival of the fittest" entailed nothing uniform either for sociological method or for political doctrine. A "Social Darwinist" could just as well be a defender of laissez-faire as a defender of state socialism, just as much an imperialist as a domestic eugenicist. clxvi

Nevertheless, the term has a certain cache, and longstanding usage, to describe tenets that were developed by, or spun-off from, Darwin'sclxvii original thesis that applied to biological concepts of natural selection and survival; and that were then extended to the "survival of the fittest" in sociology and politics. Darwin's concept of evolutionary adaptation through natural selection became central to modern evolutionary theory, and it has now become the unifying concept of the life sciences.

Darwin's theory of evolution is based on key facts and the inferences drawn from them, which biologist Mayr summarized as follows:

Every species is fertile enough that if all offspring survived to reproduce the population would grow (fact).

Despite periodic fluctuations, populations remain roughly the same size (fact).

Resources such as food are limited and are relatively stable over time (fact).

A struggle for survival ensues (inference).

Individuals in a population vary significantly from one another (fact).

Much of this variation is heritable (fact).

Individuals less suited to the environment are less likely to survive and less likely to reproduce; individuals more suited to the environment are more likely to survive and more likely to reproduce and leave their heritable traits to future generations, which produces the process of natural selection (fact).

This slowly effected process results in populations changing to adapt to their environments, and ultimately, these variations accumulate over time to form new species (inference). clxviii

When one peruses the above, it becomes quite evident that there was a huge jump in assumptions made in the original theory to applications of biological principles to social and political realms. It must always be remembered that Darwin, and his cousin, Francis Galton, who transposed the original data, were both upper-class (ruling class) members. As such, the translation of the material was intimately related to their own cultural backgrounds.

This philosophy of pretentious arrogance, and the power upon which it relied, assumed a learned helplessnessclxix in the populace upon whom they were completely dependent. This allowed the even greater malignance to grow as a template (including childrearing principles); and assume prominence as the way of life, overshadowing all other orientations, often utilizing vast economic and military power—until most people were indoctrinated to adopt the stance of wounded dogs who obeyed their cruel masters for fear of even more brutal treatment, robbing them of their dignity and inborn rights as human beings and children of the Universe

Miller noted that there is a "poisonous pedagogy," a pervasive system of thought, rooted in childrearing practices (dating back millennia in world cultures) aimed at "the suppression of vitality, creativity and feeling in the child...by the use of various coercive methods, including scorn and abuse...in order that [the child might] become an independent competent adult deserving of respect." clxx

Ideology

Ideology has been defined as: "Ideas imposed by society and embraced by individuals which determine our lived relation to the real, in order to maintain the status quo." clxxi Ideology helps to assure the reproduction of those activities that ensure the reproduction of wealth—and maintain a dominant class that controls society as a whole through owning the means of production and distribution.

Thus, in a very real sense, the ideology of commerce determines the working blueprint of ideas, values, and rules that become interwoven into, and ultimately control, society itself. Kavanagh noted that the very existence of any society is only possible because its citizens hold a mental image of it and carry that around within themselves.

The great games of modern politics, the by-products of democracy that often threaten everything democracy was meant to be, are the games of opinion molding: propaganda, brainwashing, programming and deprogramming, advertising and public relations.clxxii

Chomsky noted, "What in more honest days used to be called propaganda... [is actually the] manufacture of consent, creation of necessary illusions, marginalizing the general public or reducing them to apathy in some fashion." clxxiii We are continually and collectively manipulated in order that we retain the illusion of control, while seemingly "choosing" the most appealing people and laws.

Most people develop acceptable self-images by accommodating their values to the logic of their activities, which are in turn structured by society's institutional boundary...therefore, powerful pressures push people to seek only what society is prepared to

80

bestow upon them. clxxiv

Ideological Hegemony

Hegemony simply means "control." Ideological hegemony develops in a society when the underlying cultural biases become so integrated into the psyche of the society that they are believed, accepted, and consequently acted out by the members of the society as "normal." These values are reinforced through laws, advertising, and the media. Once adopted without examination, passed along from the first taste of mother's milk, there is no further need of outside reinforcement. People reproduce the ideology without thought or discrimination; and the cultural elites, those who essentially own and control society invisibly, make disembodied business decisions based solely on the needs of large corporations, none of which have any moral guidelines. Neither group thereafter questions the authority or appropriateness of this tyranny.

Unless the underlying bases are closely examined, most people live lives that are trance-like, in the sense that so much is taken for granted—commonly shared beliefs based simply on recall of ordinarily experience that avoid the roots (often shamed) of behavior and choice. This lack of critical examination allows individuals to think that their beliefs are the "right and proper" ways of doing, being, and thinking—thus, the person may act upon them without reservation.

Those who occupy the decisive power positions are ready to use their power to impose the traditional definition of 'reality' on the population under their authority. These ways are thereinafter recognized as normal standards by which everyone is expected to live. This type of manipulation induces trance-like actions, leading individuals, even whole populations, to act as directed by those authority figures. clxxv Such conformity can, of course, be easily co-opted and integrated into the service of the dominant culture. As Lopes observed, "Propaganda is to democracy what violence is to totalitarianism." clxxvi

CHAPTER TEN
THE CULTURE OF GREED

Our first and only duty is the development and refinement of consciousness

Argüelles, 1975, p. 279.

Definition

Greed is defined as "Excessive or rapacious desire, especially for wealth, or possessions." clxxvii I believe greed is driven by a vast, aching inner emptiness seeking to be filled externally. Such acquisitions to serve the purpose of temporarily "fixing" that craving. In this sense, it is an addiction. The hunger drives almost all of us in some way or other, driving us to devote the bulk of their time and energy spent pursuing the illusion of control, and then, continually, again and again, seeking to fulfill the failed aftermath. The key to this usurpation of consciousness is greed. Greed is the supreme addiction.

This has all grown out of the Enlightenment Project of the 18th Century. The philosophical notion of reductionism is ostensibly used to reduce a proposition to its simplest components. It postulates that if something does not have physical form, such as ideas or emotions, and therefore cannot be measured or counted, it literally does not matter. It does not factually exist—and is, therefore, unworthy of consideration. This reduction ad absurdum has promoted embracing appearance above essence. Extended to the realm of politics, such an attempt defines the very nature of delusion—believing that one might heal the inner deficiencies with an external solution. We have been indoctrinated to adopt corporate greed, and double-think; into believing that ownership of private property can, and will, satisfy the ache of the heart for true intimacy.

Greed and the False Self

This inner paucity often contributes to the grandiose, even obsessive, desire to build up of one's outer presentation—wardrobe, home, car. Commodifying everything as not having intrinsic value, but existing only for one's own personal satisfaction, ultimately feeds the hunger for the peace of mind that is the lost treasure of our birthright, what Redfield called "the birth vision," that precious aspect of self that is lost due to the multiple influences of pervasive childhood conditioning. The roots of this dilemma lie at a pre-verbal level of development, arising secondary to what Laing called "primary ontological insecurity." Shame might even cause an individual to "question the reason for this life… [And] doubt that he has a legitimate place in the universe," leading such a one to feel that he or she were an unembodied self.

The loss of intimacy and empathy lead directly to attracting addictions. This induction of narcissistic hunger lies in cultureclxxviii, and disregards deeper human needs. Acquisition of material goods may be shame-avoidant, allowing one to create a temporary bridge between oneself and the felt sense of deficiency.

Of course, such acquisition never really works, but when one has been fed a subtle program of "Net worth equals self-worth," and one is feeling deficient, it is not too big a leap to see how one might become addicted to acquisition in order to make oneself feel better; that one might actually be led to believe in the illusion.

Greed and Acquisition

Tolleclxxix spoke about "owning" material possessions as a disease, as an identification with the illusion of the separate self, the "I," or ego. Because we've been taught to make such identifications from birth, we accept it as "normal," even though it causes great difficulty as one grows older in terms of harmonious living and relationships.

This attitude extends to whatever one possesses, even one's body—a sense of identification or ownership that is related to the sense of attachment with which all mammals are born. Therefore, the loss of a treasured person, even an object or possession, may be seen as a loss of self and one may react as if it were. Adults often deride extreme reactions in children when they lose a toy or a pet; but adults react in a similar manner when their car is damaged, perhaps even more so when a friend or relative is injured or dies.

The fear here is not of biological death, but of psychological death (fear of annihilation, ceasing to exist). It is, in fact, the death of the earlier concepts of self that gives rise to a succession of more mature and hopefully more fully developed images and identifications. In the healthiest manner, this will always include re-evaluation and integration of one's closely held previous ideas.

Shopping

Shopping has become the "drug of choice" for many. In the tensest moments of September 11, 2001, a terrified and needy nation awaited the words of George W. Bush to inspire and console them. When asked: "What should we do, Mr. President?" he plumbed the specious depths of his inanity, after seeming eternities of pondering for twenty-three minutes, and disingenuously answered: "Go shopping!"

While shopping is a necessary chore, and seemingly innocuous, it may frequently turn into an obsession. It may induce a form of trance in which one becomes so absorbed in the activity that all other judgments are suspended (like the absorption that is a quality of hypnosis). The frenzy of buying (especially at the further emotional remove of using a credit card) may give rise to an insouciance about daily life activities. The exhilaration of this altered state may create the belief that compulsive shopping is a legitimate method of stress relief. Such people are process addicts, more concerned with mood alteration than the activity they are pursuing. Such people are similar to gamblers and sex addicts. It can be as addictive as heroin or alcohol. The underlying need for such activities is almost always a self-soothing attempt to dispel unwanted emotions.

Greed and desire drive most people into a frenzy of work-based activities designed to attain their goals, the attainment of which leads to attempting to fulfill more goals and desires. One is constantly assaulted by advertising for what is available, and what others have—creating even more desire, always leading to other desires, ad nauseam. This is the process of addiction nonpareil.

Greed and Violence

Violence of all sorts (against oneself and others) is intimately related to shame and rage. It depends to a great extent on the degree to which one's healthy emotions have been suppressed and/or disowned. When one is not allowed an outlet through normal neural and emotional circuits, rage may become magnified. All children are taught to protect and idealize their parents, even see them as "gods"—certainly far more powerful than they are. Children, in turn, may learn to harm themselves instead of others, suppressing legitimate anger and hurt. Children may adopt quasi-adult behaviors in a process known as dulcification, or role inversion. This deep rage may masquerade as depression.

Often individuals with mirror hungry personalities experience tremendous "narcissistic rage" episodes when their immediate needs aren't met—they experience any rejection as a threat to their sense of self and respond by attacking the source of danger. Underneath all this is the lingering risk of empty depression that reflects the sense of non-being so dangerous to those whose needs for mirroring have not been adequately met. clxxx

Even if one acts out in retaliation against others who represent one's shame (i.e., homophobic men attacking gay men in order to avoid their own fear and shame about homoerotic feelings), one will, in all likelihood, tend to avoid the area of pleasure or competence about which one is ashamed. I believe this "recycling" of the shame-based energy is what lies behind most of the violence on this planet—suppressed and turned inward, and then acted out against the "appropriate" targets. Governments use this mechanism in order to control populations as well, even in turning portions of populations against others of similar ilk (i.e., inflaming the Shiites against the Sunni Muslims). Indeed, all racism, sexism, ageism, classism, "ethnic cleansing" may be the results of such manipulation. It's easy to see how draconian political agendas and the insane focus on profit at any price could easily become addictive. There are even deeper roots that underlie these phenomena, based in a belief system to which every child is exposed, if not immersed.

CHAPTER ELEVEN
SOCIETAL STRUCTURE

Propaganda is to democracy what violence is to totalitarianism"

Lopes, 1991, p. 2.

Shaping the Container

It has been observed that children may absorb their orientation to life and the world by default through a variety of "complexly interconnected social apparatuses" clxxxi that address the individual's unconscious fears, desires and rational interests. Government, law, and media all play complimentary roles in establishing this channeling of the individual's interests by promoting nationalism, accepted business practices and customs. Since individuals are socialized to seek inner satisfaction outside of the self, this external refocusing fits comfortably into the deeper agenda of such agencies as the Corporate State.

Continual growth is the very essence of advanced capitalism, and requires a populace conditioned to embrace the constant acquisition of material goods as the premier focus of their lives, vastly more important than spiritual needs.clxxxii The majority of the populace thus controls itself in keeping within the promoted mandates, without any further need of reinforcement (ideological hegemony).

The current materialist orientation has deified technology in all of its manifestations, in order to commodify culture that both feeds and is fed by an addicted society, despite the fact that "our first and only duty is the development and refinement of consciousness."

"Faith in the existing system of economic distribution is surprisingly high. In every social group, economic inequality is not questioned as being necessary and fair; and that individuals are responsible for their economic position." clxxxiii This collective disengagement of consciousness is dissociative, and is a

Normative characteristic of modern life, directly attributable to the distancing impact of social structures that are built upon, and in turn encourage, a lifestyle reliant on advanced technology, rampant consumerism, and constant mobility.clxxxiv

The power of a culture and economy that is controlled through the malicious use of media helps create a collective "groupthink," and promulgates an "acceptable" view of what is good, right, and proper. Thus, for example, one matures, having been indoctrinated to obey authority, and revere one's abusers, (The Fourth Commandment). One learns to blame oneself in a misguided attempt to avoid shame, and thus contributes directly to ensuring continued maltreatment and the growth of Empire.

Violence and dissociation are built into the extant system. For example, as school children we are taught about the "discovery" of America by Columbus. We are not taught about the American Holocaust, the systematic slaughter of 120 million indigenous

90

people in the Americas.clxxxv The lies, rationalizations, and delusions that feed this are enormous, and are hidden in revisionist history texts and other "myths" created to defend and uphold continuing crimes against indigenous peoples that are touted as "defending our way of life" or "national security issues." The so-called settlement of the West was accomplished with lies and duplicity as well as practicing genocide (smallpox contaminated blankets, slaughters too plentiful to enumerate). In addition, there have been more than "370 treaties" made with Native people—none of them has ever been honored.clxxxvi

Genocide, rape, torture, forced sterilization, war, racism, and hate crimes, are routinely ignored, or "forgiven," by those endowed with official power. Albert et al. commented, these suppressions and violations of human freedom and dignity are often touted and rationalized as being:

Ordained by God, ethnicity, gender or racial superiority, paternalism, electoral mandate, national salvation, economic efficiency, elite competence…Elite rhetoric focuses on the "free choice" involved in voting while obscuring the separation of all crucial decision making from the populace's will, oversight or even awareness. clxxxvii

Advertising and Ideology

Advertising is based on the fact that our associations and conditioning are similar enough "that the right messages will

91

manipulate us into wanting the product...as in television advertising to sell products or, what is much the same thing nowadays, political activity to sell candidates and programs."clxxxviii

"The self is free to profit, and that capacity is the underlying, all-pervasive cultural motivation that is absorbed by members: I profit, therefore I am." clxxxix

"The consensus trance" cxc is intimately related to creation of a reactive automaticity of consciousness, such as immediate response to calls for patriotism, and the compliant response to which many people blindly respond, more commonly known as a "knee jerk reaction."

Jules Henry noted in 1963, in his brilliant book Society Against Man, "It is only the deliberate creation of needs that permits the culture to continue;" and

The average American has learned to put in place of his inner self a high and rising standard of living, because technological drivenness can survive as a cultural configuration only if the drive toward a higher standard of living becomes internalized. Therefore "Children must be trained to insatiable consumption of impulsive choice and infinite variety." cxci

We are all early conditioned (through our interactions with our parents) to be emotionally available to blandishments of advertising, disinformation, and media "spin"—creating ever-greater fear and uncertainty, allowing for the impact of buzzwords like "patriotism," and "national security" to induce individuals to respond in the "proper" manner without examining the how or why of it.

Henry called it the "Pecuniary pseudo-truth…A false statement made as if it were true, but not intended to be believed." cxcii This has become the accepted universal standard advertisers utilize to sell goods and services. This kind of deception has been used to almost create a kind of religion around consumerism, and a holy artifact about consuming goods and services. If individuals were to pay better attention to their own genuine emotional needs, they would, almost of necessity, repel the frantic efforts demanded by ever-expanding consumer growth. "The American people have been educated to put the high-rising living standard in the place of true Self-realization."

The key aim of advertising is to create the desire for more, with, of course, every desire fulfilled leading only to further desires that are equally empty and unappealing. This is the process of addiction nonpareil. Underlying all of this is the simple desire to feel whole and complete.

Chomsky noted that "What in more honest days used to be called propaganda… [is actually the] manufacture of consent, creation of necessary illusions, marginalizing the general public or reducing them to apathy in some fashion." cxciii We are continually manipulated in order that we might retain the illusion of control, while seemingly "choosing" the appealing people, politicians and laws selected by those who own and control society. We are lulled into our own "personal trances," cxciv each of us creating our own individual naïve reality that we mistake for "Reality."

This collective trance, based on the individuals' beliefs in separateness, enables all manner of manipulation, based on statistics that are manipulated to create response desired for whoever is paying. This massive effort is masked under numerous guises, such as "building the economy" or "national security" as the blanket name for ever increasing military budgets and the exponential growth of "law enforcement agencies." We have been lulled into agreement by a culture that depends on having a populace that is, in effect, asleep.

It is the collective holding onto artifacts from the past that are unfulfilled and unintegrated in the present that leads to rigid, pre-programmed views and opinions that do not allow a fresh perspective of critical thinking.cxcv Not questioning the current ideology and whatever pronouncements the current regime in Washington D.C. puts out has been so successful (for the most part) and so efficiently reinforced political and economic attitudes that many citizens never question the party line, as always announced by the most recent government "talking head"—even though living the sacred in one's daily life in technological civilization "is viewed as a crime and a direct threat to the very existence of society." cxcvi

Impression Management

There are those who contend that "Every social situation is a dramaturgical performance—subtler perhaps [than a court trial], but nonetheless an active juggling of identities," cxcvii implying that there is always some form of negotiation between any two (or more) parties to establish a relationship that is manageable. The concept of impression management states that everyone actively works to present their best qualities to others—either by a more or less conscious self, or, in the case of professionals, by public relations people such as Ronald Reagan's "Spin Doctors," or attorneys for O.J. Simpson's defense team.

This also implies the potential for locking in sets of characteristics that are "acceptable" to the parties involved—no matter what the motive (such as corporate arrangements for raping the Earth), thus solidifying an identity which may then be taken as a given and used in either promoting or dismissing an individual or idea. Stereotyping is similar, based on a presumed and prejudged set of characteristics and their denotations (e.g., racial or gender imaging). This, too, is a feedback loop involving the behavioral confirmation that one gets from others' reactions, that may create self-fulfilling prophecies (again, positive or negative); or through reconstructive memory.cxcviii

"Our preconceptions of ourselves shape who we present ourselves to be; our preconceptions of others shape how we behave toward them."cxcix Thus, there is a feedback loop that is continually being re-shaped simultaneously with its creation. In this, one both initiates and reinforces oneself through, and with, others in the interactive process.

One presents oneself to others in order to garner an exchange or benefit. It is all too easy (even expected) that one will live a fragmented life that is "functional" in terms of contemporary society— which is, itself dysfunctionalcc and not meeting the true spiritual and emotional needs of individuals, instead presenting codified substitutes through an ongoing campaign in the media to keep the populace dumbed down. (This certainly resonates with Juvenal's judgement almost two thousand years ago, of people seeking anxiously for "bread and circuses"—the ancient equivalent of television, video games and sports contests).

Functioning is not a valid measure of emotional vitality, moral competence, or as a key to healing the fractured self. In contemporary society, many people are lauded for moneymaking and fame-seeking efforts. Yet underneath the glitz and the glitter often lie tremendous unresolved emotional issues. The list of addicted celebrities, politicians, and others (often proclaimed as role models) who are corrupt, damaged, and sodden with the predilection to addictions, is enormous.

A perfect example of the fracturing in contemporary society is the disproportionate emphasis on image. The fashion industry, as a purveyor of superficial chic, contributes to many different industries—magazines, films and music. The pervasive "youth culture" is intimately connected to the proliferation of cosmetic surgery and the vast use of cosmetics that promote image above essence, especially for women. Again, this is strictly related only to the profit motive, feeding on the (often imagined) inadequacies of women, and exacerbating the unsatisfied greed of humanity. Thus, the cycle comes full circle.

The great technological fix has become the "go to" choice for every malfunction of modern humanity, often created, at least exacerbated, by technology itself. I indict the machine-like thinking of contemporary advertising models created strictly to sell ever-increasing amounts of products and services; and aimed at withholding the truth of many matters, often under the rubric of "for your own good" or "national security"—and hiding actual intent in order to manufacture the consent of the populace.

Other Artifacts of Socialization

"I consume, therefore I am" (Comedo ergo sum) might be an apt modern re-statement of Descartes famous dictum. Eating food, consuming vast resources, and devouring services have all come to replace religion (Latin "to bind back into the one"). Throughout time, religions have been created to serve the power elites as a means of social control through their ideology as well—channeling the vast energies of the masses into belief into culturally "acceptable" directions. They represent a shadow of true self-awareness and integrity, and, in my opinion, effectively replace the soul's true quest for inner peace and spiritual attainment. This insatiable "black hole hunger" feeds off of the shame-induced sense of hunger or deficiency. This, in turn, leads to an increasing desire to own and control.

Television and Violence

Mandercci spoke extensively to the "Unifying of experience" and "Lack of alternative choices" afforded by the television experience—especially in the delimited manner in which information is presented seemingly without prejudice, to brains that are reduced in frequency reception from beta (active attention, such as required by reading) to alpha (passive attention, the attendant lack of focus, and access to critical faculties).

Television addiction is virulent, and mostly ignored; or dismissed as being minor or harmless. Television's electrical broadcast frequency actually switches brain activity from the left to the right hemisphere. Moore reported that, while watching television, the right hemisphere is twice as active as the left (a neurological anomaly), releasing a flood of opioid peptides. (Opiates introduced externally act on the same opioid receptors as naturally-produced endorphins, so there is little difference between the two). The crossover from left to right releases a surge of beta-endorphins and enkephalins that are "structurally identical" to opium, and are usually "habit-forming," in the same manner that cracking knuckles, strenuous exercise, video games, and orgasm can be. ccii

Early research (in 1988) found that the average teenager under the age of 18 spends twice as many hours (20) watching television as doing schoolwork (10) during an average week. Further, "These children observe 18,000 killings before graduating from high school." cciii As of 2012, the statistics are far more alarming. Children watch an average of 4.5 hours of television daily (42 hours a week) and will have witnessed approximately 200,000 killings by the time they graduate. No matter how subliminal or subconscious, the possibility of children being programmed for violence is a harvest that we, as a collective humanity, will have to reap in years to come.

There is strong evidence linking childhood violence with learning disorders and disabilities, especially Attention Deficit Disorder (ADD), and prematurely diagnosed Bi-Polar Disorder. cciv Individuals dissociated from their own self-awareness may turn to violence.ccv Such individuals may respond from deeply-ingrained previous conditioning completely without discrimination.ccvi Other research hypothesized that dissociation may create dependence on this kind of re-traumatization, defending against trauma by dissociating into an "alternate reality," (e.g., video games) by which to attempt to regain an illusory sense of power and control. ccvii It is an old adage that "whatever mood alters our chronic pain will take precedence over everything else."

The potential for violence, like that of addiction, might seem attractive because it appears to offer relief from disturbed emotional states. Violence is often approved in a de facto manner within the culture. "Unconscious" generally refers to material that is dissociated—traumatic experiences hidden in unawareness. This material then begins to act "automatically" (as if of its own accord)—chewing one's fingernails or pulling on one's hair are examples of behaviors usually done to relieve tension or anxiety, but seemingly without paying active attention.

The Most Recent Statistics

The brilliant film, The Mask You Live In, revealed updated statistics, noting that young men's "brains are being digitally rewired" and have become "habituated to the sameness of violence."

Most recent statistics shows that:

Every week, boys watch 40 hours of TV; play 15 hours of video games; and 2 hours of porn, the total of which is clearly creating "arousal addiction"

99% of boys play video games

90% of games approved for children over the age of ten contain violence

31% of boys consider themselves addicted to video games

50% of parents don't monitor ratings of games

39% of all boys are exposed to unwanted pornography

93% of boys have been exposed to video porn

68% of boys watch porn weekly

21% of boys watch porn daily

83% of boys have witnessed group sex

39% of boys have witnessed bondage

18% of boys have witnessed rape

Research shows that such exposure increases sexual aggression by 22%

Research shows that such exposure increases belief in the myth that women enjoy sexual violence by 31%

50% of all boys are physically abused, and 1 in 6 sexually abused

Those who have been abused are 9 times more likely to commit violent crimes

90% of homicides are committed by men; 50% of them by men under age 25

Mass homicide (more than 4 people killed) occurs approximately every 2 weeks, and has tripled since 2011

School shootings happen about once a week since Sandy Hook (2012). ccviii

The question of causation, however, remains contested. What's missing are studies on whether watching violent media directly leads to committing extreme violence, though

In fact, the Surgeon General, the National Institute of Mental Health and multiple professional organizations—including the American Medical Association, the American Psychiatric Association and the American Psychological Association—all consider media violence exposure a risk factor for actual violence.ccix

CHAPTER TWELVE:
THE CORPORATE STATE—
PART I

A ll the problems we face in the United States today can be traced to an unenlightened immigration policy on the part of the American Indians. Pat Paulsen

The Etiology of the Corporate State

Since etiology is a reference to the clinical development of a disease, I believe it is germane to use it vis-à-vis the development of the Corporate State.

Corporations of sorts have existed for thousands of years. In fact, until 2009 the oldest continuously surviving business was Kongo Gumi, a Japanese temple construction business (founded in 584 CE), finally closed its doors. Guilds and banks have existed since the 16th century. Trading merchants, who raised capital to fund individual ships or voyages (some with royal patronage) were also not a new phenomenon. What is relatively new was the idea of a publicly traded joint-stock corporation, an entity with rights similar to those of states and individuals, with limited liability and significant autonomy (even in its earliest days, when corporations were formed only for defined periods of time by royal charter).

Any sufficiently advanced technology is indistinguishable from magic," but technology and science aren't what create the visible magic. It is business. And the story of business in the last 400 years is the story of the corporate form. It is the consequence of a social contract like the one that anchors nationhood. It is a codified bundle of quasi-religious beliefs externalized into an animate form that seeks to preserve itself like any other living creature. ccx

In Pre-Columbian Days

In a personal communication, Harold Dick Jr. told me that prior to the disastrous advent of Columbus, in ancient tribal societies "I am the environment" was the dominant ideology; that there was no separation between people and environment; autonomy was the rule of the day; and that everyone worked for the general well-being of the village as an extension of all the individuals involved.

Since all decisions affected everyone, one of the fundamental aspects of tribal life was a focus on reliable and effective communication amongst all members. All decisions took place within a context of trust, safety, and protection because everyone knew that they were loved and valued, and that each person had an intrinsic and necessary place within the great container of wholeness that represented the tribe.

When decisions were to be made, everyone inclusively had direct input into the making of the decision. This included taking as much time as necessary to gather everyone and discuss the relevant issues for however long it took. The law of the land then was such that leaders were judged by their success in creating beneficial outcomes; otherwise they were eliminated from positions of authority. There were no policemen to "enforce laws" or demand obedience from a reluctant populace. Right and wrong were modeled daily by every member of the tribe. According to Russel Means:

In essence, indigenous society is anarchistic, not centered around any kind of governmental or political institutions, but rather based on family. The only structure imposed on indigenous societies in terms of schedule or calendar is the one that occurs naturally—the order of the seasons of the year. ccxi

Ancient Roots

The development of perspective in the Fifteenth Century by artists marked the beginning of a pattern that allowed an individual to view an object without seemingly being personally involved ("objectivize"). Attendant to this were sociocultural changes: witch hunts, the slaughter of indigenous peoples in less technologically advanced lands, the creation of the mental hospitals, and the extensive use of slavery—all related concepts involving ostensible objectivity. In 1732, Descartes made his famous pronouncement proclaiming the intellect to be the ground upon which all existence was founded. ccxii

"Because the tools and methods [of technology] did indeed address the growing problems of survival…we came to address them as numinous, all-powerful, God-like." This was intimately related to the loss of no longer living in the natural world, and the accompanying psychic displacement inherent in "civilized life—initiated with the domestication of plants and animals, that grew in intensity with the emergence of large-scale civilizations and had developed to pathological proportions with the mass technological society." ccxiii

Sociopathy and the East India Corporation (EIC)

In business, the "Age of Exploration" (Sixteenth Century) led to mercantilist corporations focused on trade. Considering land as the source of all economic power, trade is the only way to grow value faster than your land holdings permit. It was at this time that King George III instituted the systemic usurpation of the individual rights of the English colonists via the Parliamentary Acts.

The periods 1839-1842 and 1856-1860 were marked by the Opium Wars. Essentially fought by the British and the French for domination of the worldwide drug trade, one outcome was the loss to China not only Hong Kong and the New Territories but having to make concessions about the importation of opium from the East India Company. During its early history, they were what we would call today a narco-terrorist corporation. The Taliban today are kindergarteners by comparison as the British Navy sailed up major coastal rivers and destroyed whole populations until the Chinese Emperor conceded. Under Clive:

The essentially sociopathic nature of modern corporations worldwide is easy to explain when one remembers it originated in the needs of professional opium traffickers. To see it as anything other than the expression of a criminal mind-set is catastrophically naïve. They grew opium in India and shipped it to China under armed escort until twenty million Chinese were addicted by the nineteenth century... The entire British Empire would have gone bankrupt without the narcotic. ccxiv

In the 1780s, only a small fraction of humanity was employed by corporations, but corporations were shaping the destinies of empires—until by around 1980, a significant fraction of humanity was effectively being governed by corporations.ccxv

Taxing colonial trade was one of the primary causes of the American Revolution. The Boston Tea Party was initiated as a citizen action "in opposition to the East India Company's use of the English government to enable the Company to monopolize the tea market in the colonies." ccxvi In many ways this essentially defined the business strategies of modern society. British Empire makers created a colonial structure that began spreading its insidious tentacles across the globe.

The World of Time

In economic theory, per capita production is about efficiently using time. It is not a collective and objective dimension of human experience. Two people cannot own the same piece of land, but they can own the same piece of time. To own space, you control it by force of arms. To own time is to own attention. To own attention, it must first be freed up, co-opted, coerced, or manipulated, one individual stream of consciousness at a time.

There was a process to how we have arrived at the current (outdated) economic system. First, social time was colonized by the imposition of train schedules that utilized the mechanical clock and time zones in order to coerce compliance by human minds. Newly discovered scientific principles about the nature of the Universe were quickly applied to develop new technology being applied in order to further productivity and disempower human workers. The object, of course, was simply profit. "Progress" had begun.

The equation was simple: energy and ideas turned into products and services could be used to buy time. Specifically, energy and ideas could be used to shrink autonomously owned individual time and grow a space of corporate-owned time, to be divided between production and consumption. Two phrases were invented to name the phenomenon: productivity meant shrinking autonomously owned time. Increased standard of living through time-saving devices became code for the fact that the "freed up" time through "labor saving" devices was actually the de facto property of corporations. It was a Faustian bargain.ccxvii

CHAPTER THIRTEEN
CORPORATE STATE
PART II

If you thought it was bad enough that Dick Cheney used to work for Halliburton before he took office, imagine if he'd worked there while in office, with legitimate authority to use his government power to favor his corporate employer and make as much money on the side as he wanted, and call in the Army and Navy to enforce his will. That picture gives you an idea of the position Robert Clive found himself in, in 1757

Rao, 2011.

Original Intentions

I t is important to always remember that all contemporary economic systems are driven by the greed facto and ever-greater profit making—which are, in turn driven by the shame-based childrearing system that ignores the deeper needs of infants in favor of efficient childrearing.

The original intention of corporate enterprises was to further the prosperity and well-being of individuals, but not to the detriment of the populace as a whole. ccxviii There were often strict guidelines set, such as regulating the length of the charter (one year only); or limiting profit (no more than ten percent). Even as early as 1809, the Supreme Court of Virginia reasoned that, if the applicants' object is merely "private" or "selfish"; or if it was detrimental to, or not promotive of, the public good, "They have no adequate claim upon the legislature for the privileges."

Corporations were originally obligated not to harm the public interest. Early legislatures expected corporations to embrace the same "Self-regulatory traits—conscience, morals, a sense of right and wrong—that people do." ccxix

It has long been recognized, however, that the special status of corporations has placed them in a position to control vast amounts of economic power which may, if not regulated, dominate not only the economy but also the very heart of our democracy, the electoral process...The State need not permit its own creation to consume it.ccxx

Our stories about the nature of prosperity and how it is achieved serve the cause of concentrating power, not meeting the actual needs of all. Similarly, our stories about the nature and source of security legitimize military and police powers, which serve to maintain the structure of Empire. Our prevailing religious and scientific stories, too, tend to legitimize the existing system of domination.ccxxi

The modern Corporate State has arisen mostly as a result of violent intrusions that forced war, genocide, technology, and religion onto previously unexposed native peoples.ccxxii Thereafter, it became a fait accompli for multiple generations who have matured with technology and its specious wonders to utilize such practices, with proliferating multinational corporations forever changing the face of business.

"Corporate interests control the media by defining the terms of the debates… an environment where critical debate is preceded by an unquestioning acceptance that the fundamental doctrine of the state is objective, democratic, and governed by the loftiest intentions. "ccxxiii

First and Fourth Amendments

Corporations routinely infringe upon the American public's inalienable rights to life, liberty, safety, health and freedom; and routinely impugn human rights in a variety of ways. The court has granted First, Fourth, and Fourteenth Amendment rights to corporations as "people," who have manipulated the "Very heart of our democracy, the electoral process."ccxxiv

The Courts have never investigated the fact that conferral of First Amendment rights upon corporations has involuntarily subjected the majority of people to the blunt force of the "free speech" of the massively wealthy corporate minority—effectively nullifying the most fundamental guarantee of a republican form of government. They have never explained their concupiscence in granting Fourth Amendment rights to corporations, enabling a corporate minority to attempt to unilaterally exempt corporations from laws adopted by the majority (such as Dow Chemical Corporation v. U.S. Government in 1986, in which Dow Chemical argued unsuccessfully that it had Fourth Amendment rights to privacy from government oversight).ccxxv

Corporations have also wielded the Civil Rights Act, in conjunction with the Due Process and Equal Protection provisions of the Fourteenth Amendment, to overturn laws. The U.S. Supreme Court overturned a law in Massachusetts (First National Bank of Boston v. Bellotti, 1978) that had previously banned corporate spending on political referenda. This, in turn, led to nullifying laws in thirty other states, thus, granting First Amendment rights to corporations by "establishing a legal principle of the corporation's rights" to protections afforded by the First Amendment.ccxxvi

The Fourteenth Amendment

In 1868, Congress adopted the Fourteenth Amendment in an attempt to adjudicate citizenship and equal rights essentially for former slaves. By 1871, it was broadly assumed that corporations should be treated as natural persons for virtually all purposes of constitutional and statutory analysis."

The scribe during the original Congressional hearing was a lawyer named Roscoe Scoggins, who wrote in the draft of the amendment that corporations were the equivalent of people. In 1886, this same lawyer, utilizing this disinformed notion, and representing Southern Pacific Railroad, argued in the U.S. Supreme Court that Congress had had corporations in mind when "At the time the Fourteenth Amendment was written, individuals and joint stock companies were appealing for congressional and administrative protection against invidious and discriminating State and local taxes."ccxxvii

Closer to the truth of the matter was the argument (in 1947) of Justice Black, in his dissent in Adamson v. People of the State of California.

The Fourteenth Amendment was aimed at restraining and checking the powers of wealth and privilege...To be a charter of liberty for human rights against property rights...It operates today to protect the rights of property to the detriment of the rights of man. It has become the Magna Charta of accumulated and organized capital.ccxxviii

Corporate Manipulation

Contemporary politics and Big Business have always had an incestuous relationship. A perfect example would be the General Agreement on Tariffs and Trades (GATT), originally put forward under the auspices of the United Nations in 1947, then amplified in new format by, and with the creation of, the World Trade Organization (WTO) in 1994. It was a multilateral agreement regulating international trade; and, according to its preamble, its purpose was the "Substantial reduction of tariffs and other trade barriers and the elimination of preferences, on a reciprocal and mutually advantageous basis."ccxxix The object, of course, was increased profit for large corporations.

This agreement created an increased flow of business deals and an ease of operations internationally. By forgiving old corporate debt in the billions of dollars, it also opened the doorway for increased mutual interactions between the industrial and commercial giants around the globe. By reducing the tariffs imposed by "Third World" countries on products from "First World" countries, the intention was ostensibly to level the playing field by creating more fair-trading practices, and greater investment opportunities.

The North American Free Trade Agreement (NAFTA), as a kind of extension of GATT, passed into legislation in 1994, and gutted the economy. It led to the outsourcing or wiping out more than "682,900 U.S. jobs...Exports to Mexico supported nearly 800,000 U.S. jobs in 2010, but imports displaced 1.5 million jobs for a net loss of nearly 700,000 jobs;"ccxxx it weakened the unions enormously; expanded business opportunities for multinationals; and led directly and irrevocably to multi-trillions of dollars being exported "off-shore," mostly to countries where wage controls and safety management were non-existent or derelict at best—and funneled them into the already deep pockets of the cultural elites.

The King of Spectacle Politics

Another insidious aspect of rampant corporatism is clearly visible in how 'media-friendly" politicians have become in recent decades, seemingly with politicians defining themselves through the public roles they play, as if politics were theater.ccxxxi Manderccxxxii argued that television signals are processed by the brain in such a way that individuals are encouraged to become more passive and cerebral; less able to deal with nuance and complexity; and that eventually a leader would emerge who fit those exact parameters of the medium.

In 1980, Ronald Reagan emerged as the personification of that prediction. He played to the camera, and his "Spin Doctors" presented pre-digested bites of the official "reality" to the media daily. He and the media constantly played to each other in a process of reality creation. There is a reciprocity between personal experience and the media, the latter providing "The theater in which people experience political life and define their identities, and in turn the experiences of people become the merchandise of the media." ccxxxiii

Ronald Reagan was first a B-grade cowboy actor, then an advertising dupe for General Electric (which owns NBC television, and is the largest manufacturer of nuclear industry hardware). He was, therefore, particularly adept and well trained to become the first television president. As early as 1966, he employed a public-relations firm to manage his political campaigns.

By manipulating the information presented through the media so that it was both favorable to the President, and palatable to the gullible audience, the press became a "Positive instrument of governance, a reliable and essentially non-intrusive transmitter of what the White House wanted the public to know.ccxxxiv" Despite his much-touted fiscal acumen, Reagan managed to double the national deficit during his years in office.ccxxxv

His entire presidency became a media-managed affair that very effectively diverted public attention away from his true fascist agenda. Deaver and Gergen unabashedly manipulated the media and the American public, as Reagan's administration was the first to ever purposely elevate public relations above actually governing affirming in yet another way in which contentions about the manufacturing consent.

The trend has continued in the years since, with the President acting much like a medieval ruler, making and breaking rules pretty much at will, especially where war and foreign policy are concerned. The 2016 elections provided the penultimate example—a President with absolutely no political experience elected on the heels of a campaign that spent almost $1B on his campaign (though in fairness it should be noted that Hillary Clinton spent $1.3B).ccxxxvi

Cultural Collusion and the Juristic Person

Corporate greed is related to the same hunger that typifies all addictions, a hunger for wholeness. Addiction commodifies and exploits resources and people. Fascist corporatism is driven by profit-making as much as any junkie and his or her fix.

The state of the economy is the only gauge by which contemporary society measures the health and well-being of public interests—ignoring global warming, and other elements of real concern (such as health care). "It is now almost a foregone conclusion that government should sacrifice the environment, and other elements of the real public interest in order to become more 'business friendly.'" ccxxxvii

Citizens often bear the brunt of legal machinations imposed by the courts, especially since "Absentee ownership through shareholding separates the rights and powers of ownership from any personal responsibility or values." ccxxxviii There are many legal precedents that support this conclusion. Psychopathic behavior is always rewarded in the corporate hierarchy because:

Institutions dedicated solely to shareholder return would actively recruit executives psychologically capable of firing thousands of employees, selling defective products, engaging in monopoly pricing of lifesaving drugs, denying essential medical services to insurance policyholders, and releasing toxic substances into the air and water without hesitation or regret. ccxxxix

The Prison Industry

The prison industry in a perfect example of corporate expansionism. As of 2006, the prison industry was the fastest growing business in this country. ccxl At the Federal level, prisoners incarcerated on drug charges comprise more than half of the prison population, while the number of drug offenders in state prisons has increased thirteen-fold since 1980. Most of these people are not high-level actors in the drug trade, and most have no prior criminal record for a violent offense. ccxli There are now 2.1 million people in prison in the U.S., accounting for almost a quarter of all imprisoned people on the planet. As well, 62% of all prisoners are "medicated" with psychiatric drugs.

Every federal prison has a factory owned by Federal Prison Industries, Inc. (UNICOR), a government-run corporation. These factories manufacture goods for sale to the government, paying prisoners slave wages—$0.23 to $1.15 an hour...By U.S. prison-code law, if the federal government contracts with UNICOR to make a product, the government can't take competing bids. Because of a lack of competition, UNICOR can charge exorbitant prices for low-quality goods. ccxlii

CHAPTER FOURTEEN
CORPORATIZING
ADDICTIONS

Business depends upon a vast advertising industry whose sole aim is profit; and whose total content, for the most part, is inane, moronic, and insulting to anyone with an IQ above 50.

Malecek, 2015

Creating Addictions

Corporate design creates pressure to increase profits, which means it must increase the demand for its products...and create an advertising industry to condition people to the idea that material products are the key to satisfaction."ccxliii

Hinkley noted that modern corporations routinely violate the civil rights of individuals, pollute our environment, and destroy local communities.

When challenged, they threaten workers and communities with loss of jobs. They also try to convince our elected representatives that the public interest is best served by granting companies the power to destroy even more of it. They have practically convinced us that their interest is the only interest that matters.ccxliv

Since modern corporations have no code of ethics or morality, their operative philosophies are suspect at best, and corrupt at the least. Therefore, their primary money-making orientation allows for their activities to either directly or indirectly enable addictions in a variety of ways.

Corporations commodify the artifacts of addiction. Creating the actual substances of addiction (tobacco and alcohol); providing places where addictions are practiced (casinos).

Corporations advertise and/or sell addictive substances and deny their potential toxicity—all variety of pharmaceutical products including thalidomide, Phen-Fen, not to mention alcohol and tobacco.

Corporations create and profit from institutions that "treat" addictions (private "treatment" facilities), many that support the medical model whose treatment model is well known to simply recycle clients.

Corporations "own" a share of the criminal justice "industry" in that they build and maintain privatized prisons (see below).

Corporations perpetuate the myth of "mental illness," and profit from it by owning and maintaining "treatment" facilities that use brain-damaging, addictive chemicals; and promote the use of barbaric techniques like electroshock and lobotomies.

Corporations manufacture and advertise above named "medications," often knowing that the substances are toxic in their effects as well as their "side effects;"

Corporations benefit broadly from a variety of both service and manufacturing industries that support war and the permanent war economy—arms, and all other manner of products designed to more efficiently kill, maim, or injure. Corporations also profit greatly from supplying the government with such "needs," as well as from such businesses as "private security."

The Unethical Empire

As a consuming public, we are allowed all of the graphic violence we can handle (e.g., television and video games), yet are prohibited from watching two (or more) people (of either sex) enjoy themselves making love. Controlling the sexual drives of billions of people has always been one of the key tenets of the Catholic Church. It is now one of the mainstays of the controllers of the U.S. Empire. Pornography is a hundred billion-dollar a year business. In the latest stats available (2006), the pornography industry's profit was larger ($3075 per second) than the revenues of the top technology companies combined: Microsoft, Google, Amazon, eBay, Yahoo!, Apple, Netflix and EarthLink.ccxlv

This is clearly a high profit industry that has no moral or ethical boundaries or concerns, where people are brutally exploited and commodified to make a profit.ccxlvi We would not collectively approach either war or sex in the vicious manner we do if each individual had not previously been taught the relative necessity of their being commodified on some level—from having a "regular job" to being a porn star (or worse), all of which supports violence and perpetration on many levels—as if these dysfunctional relationships were holy artifacts created under the rubric of "honoring mother and father" ad absurdam, ad nauseaum.

Technology and Excitement Addiction

The unexamined utilization of technology may produce a deadening of the life spirit, and often produces a general need to excel, or to exceed pre-imposed limits, and may lead to an "addiction to excitement" generated by a desire to feel really alive in spite of the strictures of technological society that Diamond called the "Acceleration syndrome." Living with high levels of adrenaline, cortisol, and other stress hormones may predispose individuals to "Pursue lives with a dangerous level of intensity; feeling that nothing is authentic until it's threatening, [or] frightening;" and may include "Fast driving, risky sexual encounters, compulsive gambling or spending, business wheeling and dealing, or marathon workout sessions." ccxlvii In attempting to maintain the often-frantic, consuming pace of modern life, one may begin to live in a constant state of emergent necessity.

Seeking this level of intensity is frequently associated with achievement, production, and accomplishment—and can be habit-forming. The insatiable hunger for information and the pseudo-experience of television and video games is but a facsimile of the lingering awareness of lost autonomy and authenticity. One may grow increasingly distant from the nurturing rhythms of the Earth, trees, flowers, and open space. Living as the false self then becomes a "necessity" imposed by these default choices, though the soul may continue to yearn for a fuller embrace and nurturance.

Consumerism as business, scientism as science, and religion as spirituality are the logical outgrowths of technology that always presents itself in the best possible light. It eventually becomes "The framework of our awareness..." We live in reconstructed human-created environments; we are inside manufactured goods," to the point where it appears that we are actually "Living inside our own minds...And coevolving with ourselves in a weird kind of intra-species incest."ccxlviii

This kind of "Technological somnambulism" has been collectively encouraged so that people will be convinced that technology is essentially neutral—and that use determines its ultimate value. He further argued that the use of nuclear energy moves society in a more autocratic direction because It is so expensive and so dangerous, nuclear energy must be under the control of centralized financial, governmental, and military institution. Community control is anathema... [Requiring] a technical and military elite capable of guarding nuclear waste products for the approximately 250,000 years they remain dangerous.ccxlix

CHAPTER FIFTEEN:
THE BIRTH OF CORPORATE
PSYCHIATRY

It is somehow implicit in the current psychiatric system of thought that mental health is associated with atheism, materialism, and the worldview of mechanistic science. Thus, spiritual experiences, religious beliefs, and involvement in spiritual practices would generally support a psychopathological diagnosis.

Grof, 1985, p. 331.

Descartes' Legacy

In the Eighteenth Century, Descartes bequeathed a scientific method: to learn about the complex, study the simple; learn about a germ, and you find out something about the disease associated with it. This new reductionist method was to become the dominant methodology of medicine in the centuries that followed. Then in the Nineteenth Century, "another medical theory came to prominence, again in France. It was known as the theory of specific etiology, the idea that every disease or infection is caused by an identifiable microorganism."ccl

The recognition that general paresis—a condition associated, among others, with delusions of grandeur and disturbances of intellect and memory—was the result of tertiary syphilis of the brain caused by the protozoan Spirochaeta pallida, was followed by successful therapy using chemicals and fever…In spite of its initial successes, the medical approach to psychiatry has failed to find specific organic etiology for problems vexing the absolute majority of its clients.ccli

This discovery initiated a renaissance of scientific interest in mental disorders that sought both organic etiologies and to define psychiatry as a medical discipline. While medicine traditionally used observation of detectable alteration of function as a criterion for illness and disease, psychiatry created a new criterion for disease: bodily function, detected by observing an individual's behavior. "Whereas in modern medicine new diseases were discovered, in modern psychiatry they were invented. Paresis was proved to be a disease; hysteria was declared to be one."cclii In spite of its initial successes, the medical approach to psychiatry has never yet found specific organic etiology, wanting desperately to establish a basis for all "mental illness." As Szasz further noted

If we attempt to impart an operational meaning to the concept of mental health, we find that it cannot be separated from three other basic perquisites of society: the socialization of members, the maintenance of internal order, and the preservation of meaning and motivation.ccliii

The generally uninformed (or mass-media informed) attitude of the ordinary person in contemporary society has often been co-opted to accept contemporary cultural prejudices, and the belief that there is nothing spiritual about "mental illness." Such individuals may be afflicted by bouts of anxiety and depression, periods of isolation, tics, quivers, or kleptomania. They may have been prescribed any of psychiatry's "wonder drugs." All of this is considered "normal" in today's world, when much of a modern person's autonomy is routinely subjugated to the scrutiny of, and treatment by, a vast array of "experts." Loss of autonomy is the standard of the contemporary world, directly related to the forbidding of examining the nature and quality of society itself as the source of all illness and dysfunction.

Breggin discussed "The seemingly deranged person's preoccupations" as tending to focus on his or her ontological stance—holding either an "exalted or at least a central role that seems highly unrealistic." He called this the "spiritual focus of what becomes labeled schizophrenia," when an individual is attempting to deal with the deepest problems of identity and belongingness.

The thought processes that get labeled schizophrenia require higher mental function and therefore a relatively intact brain...In most Western countries, however, the diagnosis is determined more by one's lack of personal power and self-determination.... The combination of psychospiritual passion and overwhelming helplessness is characteristic of almost all the people we label mad. ccliv

If one is born with a sensitive awareness into a world culture that treats children as commodities; and manages to retain some measure of sensitivity to his or her own intuition—then one might readily turn one's focus to ontological (Greek, beingness, origins) concerns.

If one does not have a grounded sense of one's own beingness, it is virtually impossible to focus with impunity on more mundane matters such as earning money.

Fateful Folly

Sigmund Freud was avidly seeking a physiological basis for "mental illness" in his profession as a neurologist before he became famous for his development of psychoanalysis.

Although he found the task of translating mental phenomena into physiological processes an insurmountable one, and subsequently resorted to purely psychological techniques of exploration, he never lost the perspective of his goal.cclv

"Mental illness" arises within the interlocking web of relationships that comprise societies. Families, like societies, "authorize" certain forms of pathology that are consistent with their established cultural beliefs. Freud discounted the abusive behavior of his father toward him as being "Too indicative of perversion," and blithely dismissed it as "Improbable."cclvi

Sexual abuse was a prime factor in Freud's child patients who were manifesting "hysterical symptoms," symptoms that today we recognize as PTSD: heightened startle reflex; bursts of rage; uncontrollable weeping; sleep disturbance; nightmares; anorexia; severe depression; and more.cclvii

If Freud had championed the cause of the children,

psychoanalysis would never have become an accepted and popular theory. "Such a criticism of existing society would have been too profound, and the implications for society too disquieting. By blaming the victim, Freud was effectively able to unburden the society of any need to reform or [for] deep reflection... threatening, dangerous, and true."cclviii

The "Normal" Stance

Western science has long relied upon "The Newtonian-Cartesian model of the universe [that it] takes to be an accurate description of reality...An organism that is structurally and functionally normal should correctly reflect the surrounding material world and function adequately within it."cclix

Psychology has traditionally always embraced "normal science," utilizing without question the artifacts of the currently accepted blueprint as a starting point. It is rarely cutting-edge work. As Grof noted, "When a paradigm is accepted by the majority of scientific community, it becomes the mandatory way of approaching problems...it also tends to be mistaken for an accurate description of reality, instead of being seen as a useful map."cclx

Psychology is only considered to be an empirical science if it offers measurable patterns, which is why behaviorism is an empirical science, and psychoanalysis is not. These two are different sets of data gathered through completely different eyes—" both of which are valid, one of which is empirical, the other of which is mental-phenomenological."cclxi

Szasz noted that psychiatry "Is medical in name only." For the most part, psychiatrists are engaged in attempts to change the behavior and values of individuals, groups, institutions, and sometimes even of nations. "Actually, law and psychiatry are similar in that both disciplines are concerned with norms of conduct and methods of social control" ... Psychiatry is a form of social engineering." cclxii

Power and Authority

Power has been defined as one's "Ability to achieve a favorable outcome at the expense of another; and is a quality of a relationship, not an individual." cclxiii This is defining "power over" wherein one must win and the other must lose, with the least dependent person having the greatest power. There is no operative sense of wholeness involved. The felt-sense of powerlessness is directly related to "The built-in displacement of our lives from the Earth...A traumatized state is not merely the domain of the Vietnam veteran or survivor of childhood abuse; it is the underlying condition of the domesticated psyche."cclxiv We experience "A socialization process that unabashedly trains us to mistrust our own feelings and perceptions"cclxv in favor of a Social Darwinist economic determinism that pathologizes spirituality, and elevates "Certain forms of dysfunction like workaholism and sexual addiction that are accepted as normal."cclxvi

"The roots of modern psychology lie in the spiritual traditions because the psyche itself is plugged into spiritual sources," cclxvii while "Professional power is the result of a political delegation of autonomous authority to the health occupations which was enacted during our century by other sectors of the university-trained bourgeoisie." cclxviii One of the powers granted to psychiatry is that of declaring people to be incompetent to manage their own care.

Organized psychiatry...Is provided privileges and protections that are withheld from other medical specialties...To hold and treat people against their will... [Even though] the use of diagnostic or treatment measures without the patient's consent constitutes assault and battery and is a criminal offense. cclxix

Such a diagnosis purports to measure "Deviation from psychosocial and ethical [norms]...Yet the remedy is sought in terms of medical measures...And [therefore] functions as a convenient myth."cclxx

The growth of authoritarianism has been rationalized in a variety of ways and has led both to the intensification of imperialism abroad and fascism at home. A very similar attitude exists toward marginalized individuals adjudged by psychiatric authorities to be "mentally ill," and therefore incapable of forming a competent opinion. Many such individuals have had their civil rights abrogated, been hospitalized against their will, forcibly medicated, and been given ECT (electroshock treatments), even lobotomies, without their consent. Based on the testimony of psychiatrists (and

131

their appointed minions), people are incarcerated against their will in mental institutions "For their own good," or for the "Best interests of society."

Law and Psychiatry

"Law and psychiatry are similar in that both disciplines are concerned with norms of conduct and methods of social control... Psychiatry is not a medical, but a moral and political enterprise." "Bodily illness stands in the same relation to mental illness as a defective television set stands to a bad television program." cclxxi

The concepts of criminality and mental illness are equated, and are persistently confused with each other," perpetuating the stereotype of the "mentally ill" person as either dangerous or helpless. It also conveniently gives further power to the authoritarian forces of government and allows economic status-based judgments to overshadow more humane and holistic treatment goals.

Judging a behavior to be a mental symptom entails a covert comparison or matching of the patient's ideas, concepts, or beliefs with those of the observer—psychiatrist, or mental health examiner; an established reference authority (Diagnostic Statistics Manual); and the society in which they exist. Such a notion is therefore "Inextricably tied to the social, and particularly the ethical, context in which it is made, just as the notion of bodily symptom is tied to an anatomical and genetic context."cclxxii

"The omission from psychiatric theories of moral issues and normative standards, as explicitly stated goals and rules of conduct, has divorced psychiatry from precisely that reality which it has tried to describe and explain." Therefore, "Psychiatric help sought by the client stands in the same relation to psychiatric intervention imposed on him as religious beliefs voluntarily professed stand to such beliefs imposed by force."cclxxiii

This modern conception of "Mental illness" and "treatment" has spawned billions of dollars in profit in nursing and psychiatric care; medical procedures; hospital bed space; salaries and benefits; prescriptions and medications; acquisition of land and construction of buildings; and a plethora of other revenue streams. In this sense then, psychiatrists become de facto agents of the Corporate State.

Healing from emotional wounding strengthens character and uplifts spiritual foundations. It requires daily work. It is not, and will never be, a cure in the physical sense. Healing wounds and integrating the inherent power of them is, in my estimation, the basis of spiritual evolution. Modern society thrives on separateness, not wholeness and connection. This pernicious philosophy of isolation and shame (in various guises) keeps individuals from delving too deeply into their own psyches and discovering greater spiritual depths.

Wilber's description of a "Flatland"cclxxiv worldview discards the interior qualities of art, morals, and science, and reduces them to exterior quantities only. For example, a 2000-year-old tree is not likely to be revered for the length of time it had been alive, for the many events it might have witnessed, the extraordinary amount of life it has experienced, or the many species it may have nurtured. Rather it will only be seen and measured for the number of exportable board feet of lumber it might produce, and how many dollars of profit it might generate.

This perverted logic also ties in closely with the idea of "mental illness" as a commodity. "The idea that extremes of irrationality are due to a disease is inseparable from the survival of psychiatry as a profession. If schizophrenia is not a disease, psychiatry would have little justification for using its more devastating treatments... In short, if irrationality isn't biological, then psychiatry loses much of its rationale for existence as a medical specialty."cclxxv

If one views mental aberration as an adaptive response to emotional trauma leading to habituated behaviors meant as protective functions (that may become self-harmful), then the standard against which many individuals are judged to be "mentally ill" is completely erroneous, specious, and absurd.

CHAPTER SIXTEEN
SELLING "MENTAL ILLNESS"

"Mental illness" has become a leading product of the modern Corporate State. It has brand recognition, an advertising campaign, is supported by the powers that be, and generates tremendous income for its proponents.

Malecek, 2006b, p. 103.

Preface

After WWII, a group of leading psychiatrists testifying before Congress stressed the need for additional psychiatrists in order to more thoroughly treat the rising tide of "mental illness" they had codified it with the first DSM (Diagnostic and Statistics Manual) and planned to "treat" with the newest psychiatric drugs, modeled on and exceeding the efficacy of Thorazine (first introduced in 1952), for which they were asking increased funding.

" Since the neuroleptic drugs largely interdict the nerve connections, clinically …and neurologically the drugs produce a lobotomy;" and as a result of "Chemical or surgical lobotomy syndrome, amplified by brain damage, renders people much less able to appreciate or evaluate their mental condition." cclxxvi

In 1961, it was this same group of influential psychiatrists that ultimately convinced then-Governor Nelson Rockefeller of New

York to "Create a master plan for dealing with mental illness" by committing massive amounts of money for "More modern care, research and community care" because the "Challenge of major mental illness must be met through expanded and improved programs."cclxxvii

In 1962, President Kennedy, influenced particularly by psychiatrist William Menninger, decided upon a new policy that "Relied primarily upon the new knowledge and new drugs…Which make it possible for most of the mentally ill to be successfully and quickly treated in their own communities."cclxxviii What followed was "The transfer of funding for psychiatric services from the states to the federal government, and the shift in legal-psychiatric fashions from long-term hospitalization to long-term drugging." cclxxix

Psychiatrists assumed authority in this equation because they prescribed the drugs that ostensibly relieved symptoms, and their side effects, which were actual effects of the drugs that did not fit with the proposed method of treatment. "The symbiotic liaison between medicine and the rich pharmaceutical industry vitally interested in selling its products and offering support to medical endeavors, then sealed the vicious circle."cclxxx

Community Mental Health Centers (CMHC)

The massive expansion in government spending to underwrite the CMHCs, and psychiatric outpatient clinics translated into a 6,800% increase in the cost of running CMHCs during the next 25 years—from $140 Million dollars in 1969 (US Department of Healthcclxxxi to $9.75 Billion in 1994.cclxxxii The national mental health budget during the same years rose from $3.2 Billion dollars to 33.1 Billion dollars—a 934% increase.cclxxxiii By 1999, it was $80 Billion.cclxxxiv

From the 1950s to the 1970s, training grants for psychiatrists rose to "Exceed $2 Billion."cclxxxv From 1948 to 1996, the National Institute of Mental Health (NIMH) awarded more than $6 Billion in government grants for psychiatric research, with an increase of 1,632% between 1960 and 1996 alone.cclxxxvi In 1999, the annual budget was close to $900 Million.cclxxxvii

"In 1965, when Medicare and Medicaid were enacted, the total U.S. health-care bill was $65 Billion; in 1993, it would be $939 Billion."cclxxxviii "About one fifth of APA's funding currently comes from pharmaceutical companies. Likewise, many of those who currently sat on the APA's task force for revising the DSM have also financially benefited from the industry. According to financial documents provided by the APA, over half of all DSM-5 Task Force members have significant industry interests."cclxxxix

The tremendous increase in the cost of insurance, hospitalization, and medical costs in general, borne by the bill-paying public, is a direct result of medical research. (Such research is often highly inflated, with many drugs that are on the market still having inclusions for research and development). Such costs include the cost of often gratuitous billable exams and services demanded by the medical model. Such costs for refining medically oriented research in psychiatry were ostensibly used to "Eventually discover the etiology of 'mental diseases' and thus confirm the medical nature of psychiatry."ccxc

Still No Proof

Yet "Modern psychiatry has yet to convincingly prove the genetic or biological cause of any single mental illness."ccxci There is no real evidence confirming brain disease attribution. The most modern and sophisticated technology today has led to announcements proclaiming the biological roots of "mental illness," yet the studies are often doe with client populations who have long been exposed to psychiatry's brain-damaging protocols.

In 1995, the then-director of the NIMH (Rex Cowdrey) testified before a House of Representatives Appropriations Committee. He said that "Over five decades, research supported and conducted by NIMH has defined the core symptoms of severe mental illnesses...However we do not know the causes. We don't have the methods of 'curing' these illnesses yet."ccxcii

Groups such as The National Alliance Mentally Ill (NAMI), originally begun as part of a grass-roots advocacy movement to benefit the "mentally ill," have been co-opted by Big Pharma, with nearly ¾ of their revenue provided by major pharmaceutical giants ccxciiias they promote psychiatric "medication" as the primary path to healing "mental illness."

These same psychiatric experts, with absolutely no proof, continue to promote psychiatric nosology as a clinical shorthand for ease of labelling and billing marginalizing individuals under umbrella categories. The vast expansion of the psychiatric industry has been furthered and promoted by the plethora of psychiatric nostrums, sold to the unwitting public.

The American Psychiatric Association has vast legislative and promotional departments spending enormous amounts of money to win over the public and the press, as well as state and local governments. They do so "While periodically issuing task force reports endorsing shock treatment and playing down the influence of pharmaceuticals on tardive dyskinesia—issuing authoritative conclusions to support psychiatry against lawsuits, public criticism and non-medical competition."ccxciv

While medications may temporarily mask the intensity of symptoms, the approach is very superficial, and profit driven. It discounts human values by discounting the therapeutic bond and turning psychiatrists into "medication managers" who bill in fifteen-minute increments. Like Freud's disclaimer of the culpability of society more than a century agoccxcv, these practices constitute yet another form of commodification to justify drastically reducing both the quality benefit to client and reaping inflated profit for the industry.

Health care is one field wherein it is blatantly obvious that individuals have been sold and bought the party line in terms of Western allopathic treatment. This is, again, solidly based in the loss of autonomy and shame-driven practices that lead individuals to disown making their own choices and standing up and demanding to be treated as human being, not just billable sets of numbers and statistics.

CHAPTER SEVENTEEN
WAR AND THE PERMANENT
WAR ECONOMY

C ivilization inevitably arose in a fragmented state, and under such circumstances, inevitably it was power and not collective human choice that ruled our common destiny. With no escape from the struggle for power, the world was rendered unsafe for most humane and gentle values.   Schmookler, 1988, p. 23.

The US has been in 93 wars in Third World Countries since World War II

Kohn, 2006, n.p.

The "Noble" Lie

Quintus Horatus Flaccus ("Horace") first expounded on The Noble Lie: Dulce et decorum est pro patria mori ("It is sweet and proper to die for one's country").ccxcvi If one believes that love of country (its political system, economic goals, and way of life) is worth the sacrifice of one's life, then he or she might be coerced to capitulate to such propaganda that has encouraged the young and naïve to fight and die in foreign lands, to spill their blood to enrich the oligarchic empire of the elderly, the "owners" of the system.

People are daily flogged with pseudo-patriotic rhetoric generated by the media, spreading disinformation about the glory of being in the military, and fighting for the right to terrorize and conquer other countries for their resources and/or strategic value. In doing so, one effectively becomes an extension of governmental power and identity—and thus chooses to act as a channel for that, to kill without compunction or sense of responsibility, legitimated by this higher authority to "safely" discharge one's own rage.ccxcvii

This is akin to the so-called Nuremberg Defense, enacted by German war criminals after WW I and WWII—the superior orders plea, the doctrine of respondeat superior, ccxcviii in tort law, where a superior is held liable for the actions of a subordinate. It also resonates strongly with the idea of the analog child being authorized to act at the will of the internalized fascist parent (in loco parentis).

Projection and War

Projection as a psychic mechanism in which "Intolerable feelings, impulses, or thoughts are falsely attributed to other people." ccxcix A very concrete example of this occurs whenever a nation prepares to go to war. First, propaganda begins to appear in media that paints the enemy as degraded, using images of demons and monsters often wearing the enemy's uniforms.ccc In this way, media is preparing the collective field for the coming war, justifying whatever savagery will occur subsequently. The highest "authorities" of the society legitimate this process and gives de facto permission for savagery and other acts—especially since the "enemy" is no longer seen as human. Any gruesome punishments meted, any terrible horrors inflicted, can therefore be justified.ccci

Schmookler noted that projection seems to put some element of the self, outside of the self—and experience it as a threat. The war that a harsh society wages upon the growing psyche implants a punitive introject, like a separate internal voice that condemns and represses natural impulses…The internalized war is re-externalized because continuing it internally would be too painful and disruptive of the system. cccii

By projecting one's rage onto a convenient target, one hopes to divert the force of emotional power. Americans have been collectively inveigled to live with the system that produces continuous war ever since Columbus, either unconsciously, or in utter denial. In fact, I believe it is the un-grieved collective emotional residue of centuries of genocide and torture that has led to the continuing saga of wars of imperialism all over the globe. It is only the expurgation and integration of these toxic emotions that will ever result in the cessation of the continuing activities of the permanent war economy.

The blindness of our hypocrisy derives from our "turning away from the war that rages within us, the war between the demands of our culture and the needs of our nature…Structured by the requirements of the struggle for power." ccciii

"Manifest Destiny"ccciv was another vehicle created to ennoble Empire-building by legally stealing land from the Indians and giving it away to white "settlers." The aftereffects of the lies, and rationalizations that were fed to early settlers continue to be seen in revisionist history texts and films promulgated in order to defend and uphold continuing crimes against indigenous peoples unto this very day.

One sees one's ostensible opponent "Not just as a competitor, but as the embodiment of evil…Unable to reconcile the elements within us, we turn outward to enact our drama of strife…Too weak to confront the reality of our condition, we use the world to enact a fiction."cccv

Shame and War

The roots of rage and bellicosity lie deeply buried in early childhood's unmet needs, the child being rendered emotionally impotent as a result of not being allowed to express his or her deepest emotional needs; of not being allowed to self-comfort because it would be threatening to adults and remind them of their own unexpurgated shame.cccvi This is the key to suppressing and projecting shame. No one wants to be reminded of non-integrated sorrow, sadness, and shame. This is also one of the factors contributing to the vehemence with which many resist changes. "When mothering persons have been deprived of their own healthy narcissism, they will try to get it for the rest of their lives through a substitute means. The most available object for narcissistically deprived parents is their own children." cccvii

Citizens are expected to answer calls for service, based on an unquestioned allegiance, demonstrating patriotism—assuming that people will identify with having a stake in the well-being of the country; who will not respond to the "call to arms," and not investigate its nature; and who will be moved by the "Noble Lie," and respond to its inducements enough to be willing to sacrifice their sons and daughters on the altar of corporate greed.

Hitler was shamed and severely abused as a bastard child—unloved, beaten, and disowned by his mother; and as a wounded combat vet, he felt further rejected and repudiated by the machinations of the Treaty of Versailles after WWI. It is easy to see how his long-simmering rage may have erupted in his decision to attempt to eliminate the Jews, secondary to what he perceived as the taint of his own Jewish blood quantum. This was, of course, extremely wounded and narcissistic behavior, his acting as if the world were here simply to fulfill his desires. Cccviii

Martial Conditioning

It is anger and dissatisfaction with the prohibitions of existing society that motivates individuals to participate in war. cccviii "The unregulated play of power can create not only war, but also repressive and exploitative systems of governance... To rid the self of undesirable attributes —the equivalent of an autoimmune reaction reacting as if the host were an intruder.

"Traumatic overlearning...is displacement that helps explain the cathartic function of war, the release that comes from the unfettered discharge of aggression...generated by the need to safeguard one's subjective defenses against internal threats too frightening to face." cccix This process becomes dysfunctional when the nation's collective affect is not freely expressed—and channeled into pathological activities "authorized" by the culture.cccx War is an inevitable result of this type of traumatic overlearning, in defending vulnerability viewed as weakness through the false self to survive the onslaught. Thus, one denies, and even temporarily avoids, personal responsibility on a variety of levels.

"Deprived of war as a paranoid reaction to mourning, primitive peoples evolved depressive positions. The bellicose tribes of Oceania have been in a state of particularly depressed confusion ever since the Europeans imposed peace on them."

The Permanent War Economy

Chomsky described the permanent war economy as "A semi-command economy, run mostly by corporate executives, geared to military production." With the advent of World War II, the United States government became really fascist: we had a totalitarian society basically, with a command economy, wage and price controls, and allocation of materials all done straight from Washington...The U.S. economy prospered during the war,

146

industrial production almost quadrupled, and we were finally out of the Depression.cccxi

Since WWII, a "complete consensus [has existed] in the elite culture: The United States is permitted to carry our war crimes, permitted to attack other countries, permitted to ignore international law." cccxii Since 1492, the U.S. has invoked a variety of pseudo-legitimating doctrines (such as Manifest Destiny, Monroe Doctrine) to advance the growth of Empire (most recently in attempting to "install democracy" in Iraq and Afghanistan). The making of declared enemies has almost always been along ethnic and racial lines, with propaganda almost always entailing racial slurs and demonization of the other.cccxiii

The United States military system is used both as a reason for increasingly complex technological development, and a justification for the permanent war economy (developing weapons systems to test in wars in Third World countries).

The military system in the United States is "Primarily a government-sponsored and guaranteed market for high-technology production that will intervene by increasing demand for arms and high technology production to get things [economically] going again."cccxiv Aggressive behaviors are the model for the contemporary world, based on continuous war, with escalating arms production and the constant threat of nuclear holocaust. Cr eating a "necessity" to go to war artificially supports this military system that keeps the economy afloat. War has become "A normative characteristic of modern life, directly attributable to the distancing impact of social structures that are built upon, and in turn encourage, a lifestyle reliant on advanced technology, rampant consumerism, and constant mobility."cccxv

Projection and Politics

Political systems are frequently controlled and used as a means of social control in order to legitimate rather than undermine their interests. This effectively subverts any effort to change the status quo, as the subversive character of democracy is diminished thereby. Whenever popular dissent does begin to emerge, a "crisis of democracy" ensues (e.g., false flag attacks), and increased pressure from the central command is utilized, "re-engendering a passive citizenry. Keepers of the flame of democratic principle successfully reclaim their power from those who would 'destroy democracy' by actually using it." cccxvi

By the magic of identification, the narcissistic passion for self-aggrandizement can express itself as the 'selfless devotion' of the nationalist…The infusion of one's aggressive and self-inflationary impulses into the group with which one identifies offers a more socially approved outlet for those feelings. cccxvii

Politicians generally aggrandize themselves, advertising themselves as strong and competent leaders, even as representatives of "the people's interests," in order to gain access to the collective power of the citizenry. Creating constant global conflicts of various

148

sorts keeps the focus of attention diverted from the government's true agenda of pursuing ever greater personal power and status for the privileged. Leaders disavow their shame and the pain of their unmet developmental needs while using their own positions of trust to exempt themselves from common laws and ethics. Scheer provided an excellent example of this when he wrote of George W. Bush's "gift" of 43 million dollars to the ruling regime in Afghanistan (the soon-to-be infamous Taliban) in return for their "promise" to stop growing opium poppies because it was "against the will of God." cccxviii

But how many of us voted to give that money away to the Taliban—the brutal, misogynistic, severely theocratic oppressors in Afghanistan? It was yet another act in the theater of "spectacle politics" made so famous by Reagan, a theatrical gesture to tout the specious freedoms of the U.S, and "sell democracy" in the Middle East. We were only informed about this decision long after a coterie of high-ranking government officials put their imprimatur on the arrangement, they who were ostensibly working for our collective best interests in giving multi-billion-dollar contracts in Iraq and Afghanistan to Blackwater and Halliburton (and other private contractor friends of the administration). It is precisely in situations such as these where the import of ideological control shows itself most readily.

The commitment made by our so-called leaders to the nuclear arms race was made "out of the greed of human beings who are isolated in their separate selves, and do not feel the connection to other human beings"…Nuclear industries proliferate because they provide large amounts of money, and the greed is so extensive that such people do not care what might happen from their actions."cccxix

Media and a Taste of History

The media is just a propaganda machine for the government and the Corporate State. It is constantly pushing a fear-based agenda ("Sex and violence sells"). We are constantly being cajoled into surrendering more of our civil rights in order to be more "secure" —more police, more surveillance, more intrusive interdictions, GPS monitoring, less privacy on a variety of levels, RFID tracking chips, abrogation of the Constitution and the Bill of Rights by executive order, and no genuine oversight provided by circumventing Congress.

If citizens were emotionally healthy, they would be expected to turn to a healthy government for protection, much as a child would naturally turn to his or her parents—if the parent were not the source of potential threat or injury. In this example of disorganized attachment, it is the government itself from which we need protection, as if from a crazed and violent mother! (Much the same can be said for religions functioning as mechanisms of social control, utilizing their hell and damnation rhetoric, as in the past Catholic "missionaries" offered the choice between the "Sword or the Book").

Being allowed to see live feed from the battlefields of Vietnam stirred Americans with such fervor that they effectively put an end to a very profitable war for Big Business. The Tri-Lateral Commission (TLC) is a high-level cadre representing the interests of corporations, financial institutions and other business elites globally. The TLC termed the populace's access to raw facts an "excess of democracy."cccxx Beginning in 1975, its membership set about restricting access to information, especially "To the special interest groups who represent women, Blacks, labor groups, elders and other marginalized groups—in short, those who represent two-thirds of society."cccxxi In the intervening years, news reporting form battle zones has declined from live feed to embedded pool reporters to being almost being completely eliminated.

The media coverage during the Persian Gulf War, for example, was almost exclusively administration-driven spin, promoting the war. Many journalists became "Pentagon cheerleaders" and "Served the public disinformation that was more misleading than the propaganda generated by our opposition."cccxxii

The continuous war paradigm has been called "The New Great Game"cccxxiiiwherein the US leadership had courted Central Asian dictators and strongmen, ostensibly to help stanch US dependence on the Middle Eastern oil organizations and governments. The media has continued to blare the party line ("fighting terrorism") when it is clear that we were simply continuing the oil war, having deployed "thousands of U.S. troops not only in Afghanistan, but also in newly independent republics of Uzbekistan, Kyrgyzstan, and Georgia." It's the same old story with a new set of words about the good and the bad and the bold."cccxxiv

War As Addiction

War could easily be seen as an addiction. Socrates (as cited in Sussmancccxxv) declared that wars are fought to satisfy the cravings of the body, "For the acquisition of wealth; and we have to have to acquire wealth for the body, because we are slaves in its service."

It is displacement that helps explain the cathartic function of war, the release that comes from the unfettered discharge of aggression… generated by the need to safeguard one's subjective defenses against internal threats too frightening to face.cccxxvi

"There are among us people who are tragically hooked on preparations for war…It is more like gambling than drinking, since the people are ravenous for situations that will cause their bodies to release exciting chemicals into their bloodstream."cccxxvii Individuals may seek to define their individuality, to prove their manliness," through indulging in war, about which Henry spoke succinctly:

Fear of war is anesthetized by heightened economic well-being. We become accustomed to living comfortably under conditions of impending annihilation. That is why the decision to go to war, or to the "brink," can be accepted much more readily than if the economy were placed in jeopardy by war.cccxxviii

The mandates of contemporary society are driven by attempting to fulfill the unmet needs, the warped and twisted whims, of the cultural elites—who are themselves caught up in the consensus trace generated by the sense of inner scarcity. Humanity is mostly driven to accept whatever exigencies are required to ensure survival. "If the economy were threatened by war, we would be the most peaceful people on earth." cccxxix

Healing and the Permanent War Economy

Human well-being and wholeness depend on, and exist, in constant and complex intimacy with, the well-being of the Earth. So long as we are set apart from participating in that intimacy, we are severed from fully knowing trust and security, authentic self-esteem and skillful means, the larger meanings of life. cccxxx

Yet debate about the value and worth of wealth is rare. Almost every contemporary society gives credence to economic power over spiritual awareness, and equates net worth with self-worth. We are imbued as children to seek refuge in wealth as a substitute for the birthright of our autonomy that must seemingly be sacrificed to survive. The loss is incalculable.

The massive damage we as a collective humanity have wrought

upon the Earth is just one sign of the harm we do and have done to ourselves. It absolutely does not matter how much one may insist that "It is all in the past," or "I just want to forget about it," past traumas get internalized and seek with exquisite vibrancy to be released and expressed. The collective consciousness—indeed what we call "reality" —is predicated upon just such energies and actions. Violence depends on the degree to which normal human emotions have been suppressed and disowned.

One cannot give what one does not have, though many people believe that they can be redeemed through their children. It is patently impossible. It is the sacred duty of each of us to redeem him- or herself, to reclaim the lost birthright of autonomy and sovereignty with which we come into this life

Wordsworth put it so beautifully:

Our birth is but a sleep and a forgetting.

The soul that rises with us, our life's star,

Hath had elsewhere its setting,

And cometh from afar.

Not in entire forgetfulness,

And not in utter nakedness,

But trailing clouds of glory we come

From God who is our home. cccxxxi

cccxxxii

154

BOOK TWO
CHAPTER EIGHTEEN
WAYS AND MEANS

Some Personal Reflections

Greatness is a transitory experience. It is never consistent. It depends in part upon the myth-making imagination of humankind. The person who experiences greatness must have a feeling for the myth that he is in. He must reflect what is projected upon him. And he must have a strong sense of the sardonic. This is what uncouples him from belief in his own pretensions. The sardonic is all that allows him to move within himself. Without this quality, even occasional greatness will kill a man.

Herbert, 1965, p. 165.

Preface for Book Two

Having posited shame as the fundamental principle of all collective dysfunction, in Part Two I intend to address shame as potentially beneficial, even necessary, in and for one's personal development and awakening—to develop the power, beauty and strength to express spiritual radiance. I will also be discussing beneficial healing methods that I have found useful during my long journey.

Shame as Potentially Beneficial

"Experiences of shame may call into question, not only one's own adequacy, and the validity of the codes of one's immediate society, but the meaning of the universe itself." cccxxxiii And "fear of abandonment [leads to] death by emotional starvation" and "Fear of contempt [leads to] withdrawal of love," and may create "shame anxiety." cccxxxiv

For most of us, our autonomy was not balanced by a healthy sense of shame. We were often shamed by significant others upon whom we were emotionally dependent, and internalized both the shame and our reactions to it in a toxic manner, one that carried the imprinting of the shame as punishment or retribution that was required of us because we had run afoul of these powerful survival figures. Our very existence depended upon their continued benevolence, and therefore we had to adapt to their needs—even if it means shutting down our own. "A shame crisis may develop when the child's 'boundless exhibitionism' meets unexpected parental disapproval... [Out of which] develops a concept of the [parents'] desired self...A template for future behavior and self-worth." cccxxxv Once this occurs, people lose "contact with shame

156

as an emotion that provided a good framework of limits. Once internalized, shame became a core identity and a state of being. We no longer had shame available to us to monitor the limits within which our will could healthily function…We became addicted to our own wills."cccxxxvi In addition, it disallows an individual's capacity to discover an "integrity that is peculiarly one's own…and most universal."

Alone or Lonely?

The word "alone" derives from the Old English all one, meaning to be whole or composed by oneself, a rather neutral expression.cccxxxvii Although "lonely" derives from the same root, it has taken on the denotation of unhappiness, even desolation, with being by oneself. The former implies a completeness in being by oneself. The latter almost seems like a shame-influenced denotation in that it seems to imply that there is something wrong with being alone.

Social isolation may provide the space and relative safety to inspect and heal one's wound. This may encourage social withdrawal and extend the normative isolation and separateness that are standard in contemporary machine-culture.

Loneliness is often viewed as an aching craving of one person for another, though ultimately is the craving for communion with one's own soul, for the unfulfilled or unlived aspect of oneself. It is the living, breathing connection with others that is sought, though I believe it is this same level of quality connection with oneself that is even more primary—and, in fact, colors and shapes one's connections with others.

This is hunger of self for Self, the latter designating higher purpose and personal evolution to greater wholeness, sometimes called the "Higher Self."cccxxxviii Very few are ever encouraged to do anything from the moment of birth other than follow the pre-existing rules, and meet the explicated mandates, of the society into which one is born. The socialization process is essentially adopting to an insane society. We become producing/consuming machines, diverted from what I believe to be the true purpose of the soul's unfoldment, and must therefore celebrate whatever small morsels of Light we might capture.

We must, by definition, ignore spirituality in favor of money. When one turns away from the grinding machinations of contemporary society, one will of necessity encounter many obstacles and impediments to living a life that is relatively uncluttered by the desires of acquisition.

Of course, it is almost impossible to attain the status of Jesus or Buddha or Mohammed. These stellar teachers lived beyond the mandates and obstructions of their contemporary societies. They were driven by an inner light and a numinous vision.

The journey to higher consciousness is a constant one, and, in my estimation, requires fortitude, courage, and an unflagging spirit. It is what differentiates a true seeker from a poseur—the willingness to keep on, to achieve the mission no matter what. I believe one must become devoted to one's path as fully and completely as possible—including the willingness and ability to shed the encumbrances of one's long journey, including releasing all of the accumulated emotional garbage one may have been preserving as if sacred artifacts. Ultimately, I am reminded of a line from the I Ching, "Thus the superior man, when he stands alone, is unconcerned and if he has to renounce the whole world, he is undaunted."cccxxxix

Adversity

"Was mich nicht umbringt, mact mich starker," said Nietzsche.cccxl "That which does not destroy me makes me stronger." I strongly believe in the power of adversity. Adversity has been the whet stone upon which I have sharpened the mighty sword of my consciousness. Dealing with adversity has given me countless opportunities for personal and professional growth as well as deepening my life experience. Though we may all crave a life of ease, even luxury, during challenging times, I retrospectively see that it has been life's challenges that have spurred me onward into my greatest creativity and invention. (Of course, adversity may not only test one's strength and boundaries, it can sometimes break or exhaust them. One's reactions to such an extreme is the topic of the following section.)

The way that one reacts to adversity is both a measure of one's internal wiring, of one's ability to flexibly react; and a measure of one's personal development, emotionally and spiritually. In this sense then, each of us is always being tested (by the Universe), in order that we might manage to somehow deepen inherent awareness of, and surrender to, the spiritually greater forces that surround us. In this, every individual will be inexorably drawn closer to his or her spiritual legacy, as well developing the strength and power he or she carries, learning to better utilize it and share it with the global tribe— on whatever level, and in whatever manner each of us might be called upon to do.

There are so many possibilities to be explored. It is always a matter of delving deeply within to truthfully examine the challenges with which one is presented (even though they may feel like insurmountable burdens, even like the trials of Sisyphus). If one can get to the point of seeing one's life difficulties as challenges, then it may become a far more joyous journey.

Challenge

Exercise is a good example of something seen as challenging, even fun and joyous, a form of challenge with oneself, in which one always benefits—to honor the body, to be better as a human being, to improve oneself in a contest of continuing improvement with oneself—even if failing to meet one's personal goals or desires, there is always progress. One may then compete with others as an extension of competing with oneself. Winning and losing have always been seen as measures of personal worth and winning may be used as a buttress against a shattered, damaged sense of self.

Of course, it is quite possible (actually the norm in America), to become addicted to excelling in any conceivable arena, obsessed with achieving the ideal of perfection, being better than the best, the peak of peaks, and the belief that one may do so for all time, when the actuality is that every moment is fleeting. Though often attributed to Heraclites, it was actually Plato, who once commented: "You cannot step into the same river twice. Everything always changes. It is the only constant."cccxli

At some point, one's work on self-development must begin to take on a deeper dimension; must become transcendental to the notion of the everyday self. In other words, one must begin to rise above or go beyond, the relatively petty needs and demands of ego-bound selfness, especially the malicious demands of contemporary greed-driven politics; and embrace the song of planetary spiritual needs, invoking the kind of transcendental harmony of which indigenous peoples have spoken for thousands of years, describing tribal societies living with an awareness of, and voluntary dependence upon Creator, or the Great Mystery. This necessarily speaks to adopting needs greater than one's own.

The process of building a new self, or becoming aware of the Self, may be a little like manufacturing a fine ancient Japanese katana (traditional long sword of the Samurai). Starting with the finest steel available, the master craftsman heated the blank until it was soft enough to fold. He then re-folded it back upon itself, time and time again, dozens, hundreds, thousands of times; heating and reheating; folding and re-folding, constantly hammering and tempering it until it achieved the strength, power, and resiliency that would hold an edge through enormous use and many battles without sharpening. It is said (apocryphally) that there is a sword, made hundreds of years ago and used extensively, that has never been sharpened, and yet retains the ability to cut through bone without effort. This may be a metaphor for the human spirit as well.

Overwhelm

Of course, anything that has the possibility of furthering life also has the possibility of damaging life. It is all a matter of perspective. There are an infinite number of points along the spectrum from being to nothingness. Each of us has a different point at which he or she may experience a diminished sense of well-being, or of being in relative control of his or her inner resources. It is at this point that one's inner connection seems to separate from one's immediate awareness. One may find that one's ability to "be in charge" of one's own actions and reactions fades. One may find that one acts in ways that are in total contradiction to whatever values, morals, dreams, or ideals that one may have previously held. One may even decide to repudiate them as immature or unseasoned. One may abandon oneself to whatever is most expedient in the living, screaming moment in order to stay alive—to anything, absolutely anything at all.

For example, this may account for the reaction of combat veterans returning from war, and their responses to expectations from people who have known them previously—and why they don't react in ways that are "normal" or expected. Having been exposed to experiences that are often literally unimaginable, and more horrifying than the worst nightmares most of us conceivably experience. Having lived with such intensely imprinting terrors daily, such a vet will have quasi-normalized these. He or she will be changed neurologically, emotionally, and spiritually forever— though I believe that during time the intensity of such experiences may become somewhat blunted, even lessened in impact, but never forgotten. Having been over the edge into the extremes of insanity, and experienced the absolute essence of being out of control, such a person will return superficially to the common reality, but never really either seek to be deeply immersed in it again, these individuals perhaps finding it as trifling, superficial nonsense.

This is, of course, an extreme example, but also one that can be quite instructive in its power to teach—illuminating the darkest possible reactions a human being might incorporate, having been out of control, and ultimately, at the mercy of the Universe.

Introspection and Inspiration

One may attain a portion of power related to introspection,

(Latin: to look inward). Such action may give rise to an accumulation of personal power that may enable one to look with greater gentleness and compassion upon oneself and one's inner workings. Introspection can work to sharpen one's intuition (Latin: "contemplation"). It has become a word frequently bandied about, but not really well understood. It is the direct apprehension of truth or fact independent of any reasoning process; the immediate awareness of pure, untaught, non-inferential knowledge. The more one does one's personal work, the more it is enhanced, releasing archaic, internalized judgments and other emotional baggage that might contribute negatively to many psychological states. It may also facilitate one's dreams life—what Freud called the "Via Regia to the knowledge of the Unconscious." cccxlii

Inspire (Latin: "to breathe upon or into") has come to mean "To fill with an animating, quickening, or exalting influence."cccxliii Inspiring others with one's spirit, words, or emotions may be the highest gift anyone may give. It is a direct spiritual influence given, not to necessarily influence others as to share one's own joy, brightness, love and wonder—even if others do not respond or use the inspiration for their own benefit or that of others. An added aspect is that inspiration is the most direct and powerful way to help to contribute to a shift the collective consciousness of humanity.

There is No Success like Failure

This title is taken from the classic lines of Bob Dylan: "There is no success like failure, and failure is no success at all." What is often not considered in the desire to excel—in our competitive, "winner takes all" global society—is grieving the loss of losing, or of the seeming failure to excel. The more of these opportunities one experiences, the more the acuity of the experience is magnified or amplified—and the more one potentially achieves failure. It is as if some people are conditioned to fail as a form of success, accepting and not grieving the loss, internalizing it in an effort to not feel diminished personally and thereby protecting the perpetrator through a combination of innocence and subversion of the natural instinct to protect oneself. This is called losing to win.

I must admit that there is a certain nobility, or power even—a particular flavor of strength and validation—to be gleaned from having to struggle through decades of emotional and spiritual impoverishment against virtually impossible odds in order to attain small clarities and insights—and apply them to one's own life in ways for which one must ultimately be grateful; small victories that will ripple through the deepest levels of one's soul, and enrich one's beingness on every level in daily life. Seeming to fail repeatedly, and then redeeming that loss, are both part of the same cycle of loss and gain, crucifixion and redemption.

"Our history does not reveal the limits of the harmony of mind that humankind can achieve."cccxliv

CHAPTER NINETEEN
A DIFFERENT WAY

Shame is a way of embracing cultural prescriptions of desired and undesired behavior

Will, 1987, p. 312.

Historical Perspective

History is highlighted by those rare individuals who looked inward and illuminated their lives, integrating the totality of their life experiences. Since toxic shame so constricts creative urges, those who break through are usually declared heretics, lunatics, or terrorists—brilliant individuals who have defied the existing order because of spiritual or scientific revelations that repudiated the then-contemporary logic and culture, and just would not be denied their destiny. Most have been tortured, punished or killed by the minions of the existing order wishing to suppress new ideas.

They have all been spiritual men and women, acting for the collective—for a higher and greater good than the strictly personal—in order to live the truth, they had found within themselves. Many have been marked for life by the damage they endured in order to exceed. Some might not have seemed transformed to outsiders, those who had yet to experience the initiations they had had. (Of course, I cannot "prove" any of my conclusions, but I can only extrapolate from their verbal statements and actions as any kind of support for my position). One and all, they seem to have been driven by a purpose higher than mercantile, and stepped out of their personal embodiment, as it were, to act for the purposes of a Greater Whole.

Throughout the long progression of time as we know it, there have always been individuals who have shown themselves capable of overcome great injury and adversity to proclaim the beauty of another level of awareness (or "reality," if you will). I am decidedly not necessarily talking about "Enlightenment" per se.

Some Famous Examples

Socrates; Geronimo; Nelson Mandela; John Fire Lame Deer; Mahatma Gandhi; Helen Keller; Martin Luther King; Crazy Horse; Susan B. Anthony; Osceola; Muhammed Ali; Black Elk; Rosa Parks; Cochise; Giordano Bruno; Frederick Douglass; Sitting Bull.

This list is by no means exhaustive. There are many individuals who have reached the point in their personal lives where in the common everyday "reality" was no longer enough to appease or inspire them. My thesis is that when one has become "full' in the sense of having, generally through trial and adversity, reached the limits of the conventionality of the times (no matter what era) —and needing to transcend them in order to keep making mental, emotional, and spiritual progress.

One often not acknowledged aspect of such innovative or revolutionary personal developments is the deeply felt and sincere need of an individual to forgive him- or herself.

Forgiveness, Mourning, and Creative Expression

In looking back across one's life will, it may become necessary for certain individuals to retrieve lost emotional experiences and deficits, in order to properly digest them to rejuvenate. Forgiving oneself for allowing the original injuries—and for not having wreaked vengeance upon the pathogenic people involved who were the proximal cause of one's original shame and pain, is essential. Lack of forgiveness is a loss that severely impacts one's personal ability to be more relatively devoted to one's personal growth. Only forgiveness allows space for new ideas, new inspiration, and a new reality, to be born in one's heart. Such a reality creates the seeds of new purpose.

There is a period of work that must occur, the human equivalent of fertilizer for plants—and that is mourning the loss of one's personal history. I find this to be an ongoing project. It seems that no matter how much I do, there is always more hiding in the reservoir, demanding to be released. Historically I have found that when I bottle up my emotions, especially my grief, I become emotionally obtunded, socially shut down, and severely limited in my ability to express myself on many levels. Conversely when I release my tears and the attendant emotions, my vital energy flows, and I am able to create freely, words and ideas seeming to come automatically, as if without volition, released from the prison of my own suppressions and negative conditioning.

The release lends itself to my feeling refreshed and uplifted, energized and able to expend my creative forces positively. In this sense, I am the creator of my reality, though I am emptying out my resistance to the flow of higher energies flowing through me. In that sense, when asked how I write books, I always answer "No, I don't. The books write me!"

It is receptivity that lies at the core of healing, embracing a deeper level of spiritual awareness and revelation—the never-ending journey of the soul into the infinite embrace of the Universe from which each of us originated, and to which we will eventually return.

Resistance is often seen as a badge of honor by many individuals, as it seems to reinforce the separate self—the ultimate sign of what is touted as the bedrock of individuality. Much media attention is devoted to highlighting and praising various attributes of separateness. Such mass-consciousness attention actually reinforces separateness and egotism; increases loneliness; and prevents deeper spiritual revelation. It is easy to be captured and held hostage by the initial belief in the separate self (and all the reinforcing beliefs that spin off of it). It is the essence of this separatist philosophy that drives all of the dysfunctions one witnesses in the contemporary world. Shame is the key component in many different aspects of toxic individuality.

Forgiveness and Recovery

Yet another aspect of this vast, dynamic redemption process is the rejuvenation of one's health on every level—physical, emotional, mental, and spiritual.

No matter what high level of health and well-being one might have achieved earlier in life, the advent of retirement, for example, will almost certainly bring forth an acute awareness of one's unmet needs, and unintegrated memories. The retirement years are a signal for an opportunity to reclaim missing elements from one's personal domains. As well, older age usually brings either exacerbation of earlier injuries or illnesses, or newer, age-related concerns with which to deal.

I am discovering the real magic of this level of recovery is in giving back to others that which I did not have when I was coming up, sharing the gifts and blessings I have been given through my work and struggles. It is magical because I have had to learn it for myself by deleting negativity. It is beginning to come "naturally," as if I had been practicing it my whole life. It is work, but the reward is twofold: Others obviously benefit from my work and give-away; and I benefit because I have strengthened a formerly weak or deficient aspect of myself and it has furthered my becoming the man I want to be. (Obviously I am not "done," in the sense of being totally complete. I am still triggered by old shadow materials that leach to the surface to be healed).

As a result of my being clean from cocaine for 37 years, I have had to make peace with my many addictive experiences and be thankful that I have gotten what I needed from it. I truly have no desire to indulge in such a way ever again. My process led me to having to embrace the sometimes-excruciating work of loving myself in large and small ways, the most difficult task I have ever undertaken.

This has had, perforce, to include embracing and loving all of the years of struggle and pain; all of the self-repudiation and self-disavowal for perceived and actual errors and transgressions. Most importantly for my current directions: I have obtained a strengthening of my purpose, as well as a renewed resource to fuel my life-direction in embracing the ever-new possibilities for renewal and refreshment. It has required the willingness to trust enough to open up to the far-more powerful influences of the Universe; and absorb the deeply connected and wisdom-infused teachings that could only come to me because I was available to receive them.

I believe that there are levels of consciousness that one may only enter once one has (even temporarily and/or substance induced) experienced the obliteration of both one's belief in, and lived-experience of, the separate self and any idea of control. One must surrender utterly to the needs of the Universe. The example I noted earlier of the returning combat soldier is perhaps one of the most extreme.

Extraordinary epiphanies may be achieved in other ways as well—all of them requiring that one experience an occasion (or numerous ones, as required) wherein what one believes to be one's limits are completely erased. I also believe that there are a tremendous (probably uncountable) number of altered states that portend the Great Awakening to the totality of consciousness that precede it as harbingers of that embracing wholeness.

The Next Larger View

I believe that there is a larger picture to be considered. Given the addiction like nature of society, we are all addicts in one way or other. This is certainly true of the deep greed base that informs (especially Western) society, and the production/consumption paradigm in which most of us live.

In that sense, the addictive model may then apply broadly to just about anyone—especially anyone who seeks to rise above the abysmal level of consciousness that is considered "normal"; and even more so for spiritual aspirants who seek to awaken to their own autonomy and authenticity. In this sense, then, what Twelve Step programs call "hitting bottom" also applies to people who are bottoming out on their life circumstances (provided that they are living with maximum intensity), and meet the boundaries of their comfort zone face-to-face at 100 MPH. One may certainly bottom out without ever having become addicted to drugs or alcohol, to work or sex. It may be fairly rare, especially given the relative ease with which one may attain such blandishments with which to be distracted from oneself—the process is the same regardless. "Hitting bottom" implies that one has run out of options, having pushed whatever lifestyle choices one has made to the limit; and finding oneself more or less relatively helpless to continue in the same trajectory, seeks earnestly for a newer, better way, choosing (or seemingly being forced) to abandon the old ways. This parallels the experience of extreme states or situations previously described. Hence, it may become available to any and all who seek some form of transcendental awakening.

CHAPTER TWENTY
BEYOND CULTURAL NORMS AND FORMS

I ndeed, nature is more suggestive of a mother juggling resources to ensure each family member's welfare as she works out differences of interest to make the whole family a cooperative venture, than of a rational engineer designing perfect machinery that obeys unchangeable laws   Sahtouris, 1989, p. 25.

Authenticity and the Self

Authentic is defined as: "Having the origin supported by unquestionable evidence" (Greek: "original, primary")."cccxlv This original definition is in total opposition to the dysfunctional ethos that has been adopted by countless generations of the citizenry by the growth of corporatism, and the insistence on money and "progress" that has diminished taking personal pride in fine craftsmanship. In the same way, this virulent impersonal approach has fostered and encouraged the diminution of the authentic self.

This, of course, depends upon each individual having developed a sense of self-value (or "spiritual net worth") that is completely divorced from the monetary equivalent so often used in the contemporary world to measure value. It is related to creating real power in tune with the divine and eternal forces versus that which is granted by governments and institutions as a reward for obeying, and being subservient to, the transitory and arbitrary laws and rules of contemporary society. This might be seen as sharing power with the Universe as compared to having temporary power over others (this latter often characterized as "control"). This also marks the line between having a job and real work—the former related to the false self, and the latter to the authentic self.

As discussed, we have been collectively coerced into supporting a martial culture masquerading as benevolent that constantly finds excuses for and justifies for war, very much like a junkie and his or her drug. One cannot begin to recover until one has truly "hit bottom," no longer struggling vaingloriously to prove how great and important is one's own ego.

It is at that point, I believe—when one is relieved of artifice and manifests the simple glory of one's essence—that one may access all of one's inborn gifts and share them without fear. And I know that it is the work of each individual to find peace within themselves. This, then will create that great peace we all seek, as Ghandi once reflected. I pray this time comes soon for our planet

Until an individual is willing and able to understand and intimately embrace, all that one is, moving forward as a conscious individual with ideals of cultural wholeness, and a vision of a united humanity, will one be able to go about the business of transforming society as a whole.

Transformation and the Alchemy of Art

Jung wrote: "Everyone carries a shadow, and the less it is embodied in the individual's conscious life, the blacker and denser it is."cccxlvi

Miller said: "The absence or presence of a helping witness in childhood determines whether a mistreated child will become a despot who turns his repressed feelings of helplessness against others, or an artist who can tell about his or her suffering." Such a witness will be instrumental in confirming one's perceptions and "thus making it possible to recognize that [I] had been wronged." cccxlvii I definitely used my writing as a kind of "sympathetic witness" to survive my childhood.

Abreaction and Catharsis

Abreaction is "A release or discharge of emotional energy following the recollection of a painful memory that has been repressed...and may lead to a catharsis."cccxlviii "Everyone carries a shadow, and the less it is embodied in the individual's conscious life, the blacker and denser it is."cccxlix

This work is a form of alchemy, which Malouin defined as "The chemistry of the subtlest kind,"cccl whose methods would allow the creation of extraordinary chemical reactions at a faster pace than Nature, and to develop profound powers. Such work on the self is always reflected in one's daily interactions with others. It is, of course, a metaphorical description of transmuting one's base emotions—fear, anger, shame, rage—into the gold of "higher" emotional octaves—joy, bliss, peace.

Cathartic work has been an essential aspect of my personal recovery, though this work is best done after "safety, self-care, and sobriety" have been firmly established.

Narrative heals personality changes only if the survivor finds or creates a community of listeners for it. The listeners must be strong enough to hear the story without injury. The listeners must also be strong enough to hear the story without having to deny the reality of the experience or to blame the victim. To be trustworthy, a listener must be ready to experience some of the terror, grief, and rage that the victim did. To achieve trust, listeners must respect the narrator. Respect also means refraining from judgment.cccli

The Importance of Transformative Tears

Crying is one of the most highly shame-based arenas for men, completely at odds with culturally approved images. "American military culture in Vietnam regarded tears as dangerous but above all as demeaning, the sign of a weakling, a loser...to weep was to lose one's dignity among soldiers in Vietnam."ccclii This was totally in keeping with the culturally approved image of a "real man," who was emotionally unavailable and impervious. This

177

attitude reinforced the idea of "corporately-inspired warfare," which judged the value of combat soldiers only by their continuous production of body count and which was fueled by an utter lack of empathy and disallowed emotions.

Crying and releasing emotion is tremendously beneficial for healing, especially when appropriately linked to pernicious memories. These tears are richer in released toxins than normally occurring basal lubricating tears or tears provoked by irritants.cccliii

Anderson lists nine categories of benefits to be derived from weeping, summarizing what may be most essential as follows: "One of the most unique aspects of the characteristics of transformative weeping is the explicit descriptions of physical/mental/spiritual integration taking place in the context of sacred tears. Integration, re-integration, unification, reclaiming and healing of the Self, are phrases commonly used by both historical writers and interviewees." cccliv

Even before I understood the deeper ramifications of emotional release, I sought the refuge of deep release of dysphoric emotions, fear, and shame, through crying. I have generally cried alone, though I have found the experience of being emotionally vulnerable in the presence of others in a safe environment, to be amazingly powerful in deepening my trust of both myself and others. It is the ability to utterly release stagnant or archaic emotions that opens the doorway to deeper refreshment and healing.

Writing

My ability to write developed as a result of wanting so desperately have someone with whom to communicate; as a vehicle to ally my fears and soothe my nerves; to help me maintain what little sanity I ever experienced; and eventually, to taste the worlds of the invisible Universe that lay beyond my senses.

Writing was always my best opportunity to express myself truthfully; the only chance I had to speak my own truth without being judged or ridiculed. It has been my sacred haven, the only place I could go with my deepest fears and shame; feel them, hold them within myself, and release them like a flock of wild and caged birds. When I write, I can be anyone I want, feel what I want. I can escape the dross and horror of everyday life; I can flee to the most far-off lands; I can be the hero of the greatest and most exciting stories ever told; I can be tall and thin and handsome; I can rescue beautiful women; I can be the savior of thousands, praised and loved and desired; I can be anybody I want; I can be God for just a little while, in control of everything and everyone I create; I can be perfect, exactly the way I want it to be. All the time, always.

In this vein, I so very much resonate with Nin:

We write to taste life twice, in the moment, and in retrospection. We write, like Proust, to render all of it eternal, and to persuade ourselves that it is eternal. We write to be able to transcend our life, to reach beyond it. We write to teach ourselves to speak with others, to record the journey into the labyrinth. We write to expand our world when we feel strangled, or constricted, or lonely. We write as the birds sing, as the primitives dance their rituals. If you do not breathe through writing, if you do not cry out in writing, or sing in writing, then don't write, because our culture has no use for it. When I don't write, I feel my world shrinking. I feel I am in a prison. I feel I lose my fire and my color. It should be a necessity, as the sea needs to heave, and I call it breathing.ccclv

Like a Hero's Journey

The journey through addiction and recovery is emblematic of the entire spectrum of human self-abuse based on shame and recovery of the essential selfness originally lost in the process. Early on, Campbell explicated the Hero's Journey as a path to re-orienting individuals to embracing a journey to reclaim lost, innate higher states. One sets out seeking personal aggrandizement and encounters tremendous obstacles (the descent); one is overwhelmed by them and is "forced" to surrender (the ordeal); and then one is initiated into a new way of being, reborn with gifts to return to one's world (ascent). One returns with treasures like Jason, who initially thought the Golden Fleece were for his personal use, but then realized it was for the upliftment of his people. He was merely the vessel to deliver it. The initiation process through which he had gone changed him in subtle, and not so subtle ways, yet curiously left him the same. He was always a hero. He just needed adversity to test his mettle and prove his gold.

recovery from substance dependence has been a precursor for my personal recovery from the toxic effects of Western Civilization. "Working back to the causes of addiction and removing them [as] a manifestation of unconscious patterns… [one may be] enabled to live a whole and full life on this planet…a person…Transcending compulsive behaviors."ccclvi

I believe it is only by taking personal responsibility for all of one's actions, (assumed and implied, even without empirical proof), that one can become more empowered to step forward as a more fully conscious human being, as a standard bearer for all of humanity and a steward of the planet—cultivating a voluntary dependence on the Earth and her fruits, and continually asking and giving thanks for the bounty of a gracious Creator. Argüelles spoke eloquently to this:

We may approach a mode of behavior in which the expressive function of the human organism is so indissolubly wedded to an intuitive knowledge of the laws governing the creation and maintenance of the world that our least response is pregnant with a vitality and a meaning of which mechanized existence has long deprived us.ccclvii

Cultural Revolution

Dekker addressed the immanent cultural shift as deeply involving art and media, an ideological shift based on a growing deeper awareness. ccclviii Shaw once commented:

"I am, and always have been, a revolutionary writer, because our laws make law impossible; our liberties destroy all freedom; our property is organized robbery; our morality is an impudent hypocrisy; our wisdom is administered by inexperienced or mal-experienced dupes; our power wielded by cowards and weaklings; and our honor false in all its points. I am an enemy of the existing order for good reasons. ccclix

Erich Fromm, the brilliant psychoanalyst, spoke succinctly about the relationship between art and society:

All great art is by its very essence in conflict with the society with which it coexists. It expresses the truth about existence regardless of whether this truth serves or hinders the survival purpose of any given society. All great art is revolutionary because it touches upon the reality of man and questions the reality of the various transitory forms of human society. ccclx

"Transitory" does indeed describe all the forms of truth, reality, even God, as defined by the temporary definitions of passing cultures. Those topics deemed to be ancient history were, in their day, once as important, commanding, and revered as our own current forms.

Now in my seventh decade, I have entered a time that will allow me my greatest spiritual growth and grant me the opportunities to make the most positive contributions to myself and humanity. Freed of the grinding necessity of making money, I may now more freely express my true heart-felt needs and desires with the greatest generosity and focus. Anything that stands in the way of such expression will therefore simply become fuel for the fire of personal growth and inspiration for me, to write about further clearing and integrating my own deepest discoveries and to contribute to the spiritual revolution taking place at this amazing time in history.

Roszak drew a parallel to the social unrest of our own times, when he commented:

Cultural creativity is always the province of minorities. My conviction is that those who contribute to the process of creative disintegration have diagnosed the ills of the age more keenly than the official experts, or the professional planners, or the heavy revolutionaries.

They are in touch with something contagiously and constructively idealistic. But their impact on our future, on the tastes and values of our society, will never be gauged by nose-counting sociology. Nor can they expect their efforts to be acknowledged or encouraged in the cultural mainstream, any more than we could have expected even the keenest political minds of dying Rome to recognize in their day that the next chapter in Western history would be written by the scruffy and uncivil likes of a St. Anthony ruminating in the wilderness, working, praying, building a new society out of the sweat and rubble beyond the horizons of their age.ccclxi

Cooperation, not Competition

In Western Civilization, we have become completely engrossed in an orgy of machine technology. Industrial inventions amplify and mimic some aspects of human intelligence (intellectual and cognitive) while abandoning others (the emotional and the spiritual). This materialist orientation has given rise to the deification of technology in all of its manifestations.

"In classical Newtonian mechanics, time plays no fundamental role…but in the thermodynamic processes 'time's arrow' is absolutely central" … "The problem was not that these early conceptions were wrong. Aspects of the physiosphere do indeed act in a deterministic and mechanistic-like fashion…rather it was that these conceptions were partial."ccclxii

Lovejoy spoke of a great chain of beingness, in which everything is locked into an enormous network of mutually interdependent orders abiding in Spirit. He remarked that this worldview "has been the official philosophy of the larger part of civilized humankind throughout most of its history." ccclxiii "We exist in fields within fields, patterns within patterns, contexts within contexts, endlessly."ccclxiv

The human body is a perfect example. Sahtouris exquisitely described how the different organ systems of the body manage to work together cooperatively, despite being distinct entities with completely different compositions and functions within the comprehensive whole of the human form. ccclxv

Wilberccclxvi presented a cosmology he referred to as the "Great Nest of Being, with each senior dimension enveloping and embracing its juniors, much like a series of concentric circles or spheres." Wilber noted: "All developmental and evolutionary sequences that we are aware of proceed by hierarchization, or by orders of increasing holism—molecules to cells to organs to organ systems to organisms, for example."ccclxvii

Much the same analogy might be drawn for the potential wholeness or cooperation of humanity, with each nation or people retaining their unique characteristics, qualities, cultures, and ways-of-life, yet all working toward and for the greatest good of the comprehensive whole of the Planetary Being.

Mander spoke to the process of evolution as one in which we as humans interacted with nature for millions of years—whereas the current culture (driven by technology for only the past few hundred years) has been pushing humanity to coevolve with the machines we have created to ostensibly grant us more leisure and ease. "It's a kind of in-breeding that confirms that nature is irrelevant to us... [A] New World Order suggests that international bankers and developers can now literally map the world's resources and plot the flow of development according to a larger plan for an ultimate techno-paradise,"ccclxviii while "archaic cultures constitute an inner technology [for spiritual growth]…such as alchemy, shamanism, and yoga."ccclxix

The Possibility of an Ecstatic Society

Wilber's series of concentric circles of gradually increasing levels of beingness and responsibility illustrate the pre-configuration of levels of beingness and experience that are perfectly necessary and, is therefore, necessarily perfect. Each must be experienced exactly for what it is and what it contains, before one can move on to the next, more inclusive level. Wilber noted "Research tends to suggest that a general competence needs to be established at each major wave in a stream in order for its successor to emerge."ccclxx This is the sense of completion that is most often missing in the frantic pursuits and voracious material hunger of most people in Western Civilization, indeed the planet, at this time.

It is only possible to integrate this type of wholeness because it already exists. "There is a structure inherent in things, us, the world, which maximizes energy…not a structure that is imposed from without, but one which emerges from within when the blocks are removed." ccclxxi Bohm spoke eloquently to this, when he referred to the:

Implicate Order exists as an ultimate physical substrate that underlies our present perception of reality. Although the parts appear to be distinct from the whole, in fact, because they "enfold" or include the whole, they are identical with the whole. If we could invoke the precedent of quantum mechanical indefinability, we could leap to the idea of a united entity encompassing all space and time in which each part contains the whole and is identical to it.ccclxxii

Healthy self-care is often overlooked in the frantic contemporary worldview, not only of the body, but of the heart and the spirit. This requires doing the deep, inner work of healing and integrating the internalized effects of shame-based childrearing and cultural conditioning. As a result of a spiritual awakening, one may then be able to arrive at a position of truly loving both self and others—appreciating all and everything as unique, and worthy of love and respect within the vast web of Creation. This may develop as an outgrowth of recovery from addiction; the true soul work that is like a Hero's Journey; of psychotherapy; or any number of other paths leading Home. "As we own our rejected parts, we become whole and self-connected. We restore our original 'I Amness'. We must accept every part of ourselves with unconditional positive regard if we want to feel complete." ccclxxiii

This must include the world of work, which may then become the truest expression of one's inner world and potentially, even one's joy.

Job vs. Work

Each of us is birthed into a world order that insists that we need to "fit in"; that we sacrifice our precious autonomy in order to not alienate ourselves from the vast dysfunctional tribe of humanity. Attempting to please our ostensible caregivers, we abandon ourselves and are all sullied by the encrusted shame and degradation of millennia's-old imprinting embodying the emotional equivalent of blackmail.

Some parents use shame purposely to attempt to control their children. In ancient times, when everyone lived in cooperative societies and depended upon one another for provision of good and services and the collective management of resources, being ostracized or driven from the tribe was tantamount to death and was greatly feared as the ultimate punishment. Despite the opposition of a long-entrenched and dysfunctional definition of "work," it is possible that

We may approach a mode of behavior in which the expressive function of the human organism is so indissolubly wedded to an intuitive knowledge of the laws governing the creation and maintenance of the world that our least response is pregnant with a vitality and a meaning of which mechanized existence has long deprived us.ccclxxiv

Everyone, even the most venal of businessmen and politicians, is born with the inherent possibility of embodying great awareness and spirituality. Most human creativity is routinely hijacked by economic considerations, and the need to "make a living" within the context of the transient contemporary mandates—though it must not necessarily be so. Roszak addressed this possibility:

All of us have a gift, a calling of our own whose exercise is high delight, even if we must sweat and suffer to meet its demands. That calling reaches out to find a real and useful place in the world, a task that is not a waste or a pretense. If only that life-giving impulse might be liberated and made the whole energy of our daily work, if only we were given the chance to be in our work with the full force of our personality, mind and body, heart and soul…What a power would be released into the world! A force more richly transformative than all of industrial technology.ccclxxv

This is the kind of work that would, could, even should enrich not only to ourselves, but the entire planet. It involves investing ourselves with pride and grace in our accomplishments, sharing them freely with others, and allowing the entire Universe to work through each of us as channels rather than slaving away egotistically trying to reinforce our separateness.

A Partial (and Incomplete) View

"Personal experience and functioning are constantly being structured and constructed from ongoing interaction with the interpersonal, social and cultural environment."ccclxxvi Since the majority of us spend a significant portion of our everyday lives in thrall to the necessity of "making a paycheck," work should/could be a powerful, enriching experience. We could all be involved in soulful work.

Soulful work has a healthy narcissistic quality. We see ourselves reflected in our work and we grow in self-love as we see our work accepted by valuing, and self-transcendence. All three of these are necessary for work to be soulful. Each contributes to the formation of character, and from a Buddhist point of view, the soul value of work depends on whether or not it contributes to the purification of human character.ccclxxvii

This type of work embodies a deep connection with one's own roots and presence, invoking a kind of organic wholeness developed through spiritual or psychotherapeutic integration. This wholeness may ultimately invoke the experience of ecstasy because:

True ecstasy unites the intellect, emotions and action in a climax where no one power is limited by another. They are not expressed consecutively but simultaneously, and each to its utmost capacity. Ecstasy is their transitory, inimitable collision at the moment of their fullest unfoldment, [available] only by entering the process.ccclxxviii

The revivification and transformation of society can only come about through "The deliberate choice to work to reconstruct the collective structures of power which determine our lives,"ccclxxixbecause it is always the individual who empowers institutions. By becoming a living embodiment of all that one holds to be true and beautiful, one is able to model continuous transformation within one's self. In this way, one's every breath becomes a revolutionary act.

Joy is Our Birthright

And comes to rest that Godless search, tormented and tormenting…gone the madness of a life committed to uncare, and gone the tears and terror of the brutal days and endless nights where time alone would rule. And I—I rise to taste the dawn and find that love alone will shine today. And the Shining says: to love it all, and love it madly, and always endlessly, and ever fiercely, to love without choice and thus enter the All, embracing the only and radiant Divine: now as Emptiness, now as Form, together and forever, the Godless search undone, and love alone will shine today.

ABOUT THE AUTHOR.

Stefan J. Malecek, Ph.D.

Dr. Stefan J. Malecek has worked extensively with Trauma-affected clients, including 100% PTSD Veterans. He spent nearly 2 decades working on in-patient psychiatric care units in the San Francisco Bay area and nearly a decade in community mental health out-patient facilities, followed by 5 years in a private psychotherapy practice. He taught psychology at the community college level for 7 years.

He is the author of the acclaimed Paul Marzeky Mystery series: *Crazy Tales of Combat Psychiatry, Unwitting Witness, Alchemy's Angels, Spirals of Time, The Gilded Edges Of Shadow and his latest, Excelsior*. The Crucible of Shame: Healing the Societal Roots of Addiction and "Mental Illness" and Trauma and Transformation are his first published non-fiction books.

All are available now at: amazon.com/author/stefanjmalecek/

Dr. Stefan J. Malecek was born in St. Louis, Missouri, and left there in 1966 after high school to join the US Army. He initially trained as a Combat Medic at Fort Sam Houston, Texas, and worked as Social Work/Clinical Psychology Specialist at Fort Riley, Kansas. After a year there, he was transferred to Vietnam. He spent 1968-1969 in-country partly with the 14th General Dispensary/85th Evac Hospital, and then flying all over "I" Corps with the 326th Medical Battalion of the 101st Airborne Division, doing interview evaluations, and counseling many men, often fresh from battle.

Stefan returned to school and got his BA from New College in 1992, and soon thereafter moved to the Oregon Coast. He continued to work in various aspects of mental health and got his master's degree from the Institute of Transpersonal Psychology in 1998; and a Ph.D. in Psychology from Saybrook University. His graduate work was devoted to recovery from trauma, addictions and dissociation.

Learn about the Author at his website:

https://www.stefanjmalecek.com/home-page

Get A Complimentary Therapy Session with Dr. Stefan

 https://www.stefanjmalecek.com/therapy

REFERENCES

[i]Kotulak, R. (1997). Inside the Brain. Kansas City, MO: Andrews McNeel.

[ii]Morowitz, H.J. (1981). Rediscovering the Mind. In D.R. Hofstadter & D.C. Dennet (Eds.), The Mind's I: Fantasies and reflections on Self and Soul. New York, NY: Basic Books, p. 39.

[iii]Meade, M. (2002). The Gift and the Wound: Presentation: May 16-17, 2002. Portland, OR.

[iv]Freud, S. (1965). The Interpretation of Dreams. New York: Avon. Original published 1900.

[v] Rank, O. (1993). The Birth of Trauma. Dover Books: Mineola NY. Original published in German 1924 and English 1929. P. xxiii.

[vi] Tart, C. T. (1999). Waking Up. Boston MA: Shambhala.

[vii] Berger, P., and Luckman, T. (1967). The Social Construction of Reality. New York NY: Doubleday Anchor.

[viii] Butler, L, Duran, R., Jasiukaltis, P., Koopman, C. and Spiegel, D. (1996). Hypnotizability and Traumatic Experience: A Diathesis-Stress Model of Dissociative Symptomatology. American Journal of Psychiatry, 153 (7), pp. 42-63.

[ix] Freud, S. (1961). The Economic Problem of Masochism. In J. Strachey (Ed.), Standard Edition of psychological Works of Sigmund

Freud, p. 156. London, UK: The Hogart Press & The Institute of Psychoanalysis. (Original work published in 1924).

[x] Malon, D., Paulus, M., and Hurley, W. (1994). The Interacting Self: Its developmental and phenomenological Aspects in Psychotherapy. Journal of Contemporary Psychotherapy, 24(1), p. 52.

[xi] Bradshaw, J. (1988). Op cit.

[xii] Meade, M. (2002). Op cit

[xiii] Miller, A. (1990a). Banished Knowledge: Facing Childhood Trauma in Creativity and Destructiveness. New York NY: Doubleday, p. 33.

[xiv] Winnicott, D.W. (1965). Ego Distortion in Terms of True and False Self. In D.W. Winnicott (Ed.), The Maturational Processes and the facilitating Environment. New York NY: International Universities Press. Pp. 140-152.

[xv] Bradshaw, J. (1988b). John Bradshaw: On the Family. Deerfield Beach FL: Health Communications Inc. p. viii.

[xvi] Tart, C. (1988). Op cit. p. 86.

[xvii] Masters, W., Schwartz, M. & Galperin, L. (1993). Pulling the Pieces Together: An Integrative Approach to Treating Sexual Trauma, Sexual Compulsivity, and Dissociative Disorders. Unpublished manuscript, p. 6.

[xviii] Liberating Theory. (1986). Albert, M., Cagan, L., Chomsky, N., Hahnel, R., King, M., Sargent, L., & Sklar, H. Boston, MA: South End Press, p. 20.

[xix] Bowlby, J. (1983). *Loss* (Attachment and Loss Series, Vol. 3). New York, NY: Basic Books, p. 117.

^{xx} Ibid.

^{xxi} Liotti, G. (1999a). Disorganization of attachment as a model for understanding dissociative pathology. In J. Solomon, & C. George (Eds.), *Attachment disorganization* (pp. 291-317). New York, NY: Guilford Press.

^{xxii} Lyons-Ruth, K. (1999). Two-person unconscious: Intersubjective dialogue, interactive relational representation, and the emergence of new forms of relational organization. *Psychoanalytic Inquiry, 19*, 576-617.

^{xxiii} Lyons-Ruth, K. (2001a). The Two-Person Construction of Defenses: Disorganized Attachment Strategies, Unintegrated Mental States and Hostile/Helpless Relational Processes. *Psychologist Psychoanalyst, 21*(1), 40-45.

^{xxiv} Hyams, H. (1994). Shame: The Enemy Within. *Transactional Analysis Journal, 24*(4), p. 237.

^{xxv} Howell, E. F. (2003). Narcissism, a Relational Aspect of Dissociation, Journal of Trauma & Dissociation, 4: 3, p. 56.

^{xxvi} Blizard, R. (2003). Ibid.

^{xxvii} Blizard, R.A. (2003). Op cit., p. 37 & p. 42.

^{xxviii} Ogawa, J. R., Sroufe, L. A., Weinfeld, N. S., Carlson, E. A., & Egeland, B. (1997). Development and the fragmented self: Longitudinal Study of Dissociative Symptomatology in a Non-Clinical Sample. *Development and Psychopathology 9*, p. 871.

^{xxix} Sands, S. (1994). What is dissociated? *Dissociation, 7*(1), pp. 148-149. 196

^{xxx} Miller, A. (1990a). Op. cit., p. 2-3.

^{xxxi} Tomkins, S. S. (1962-1963). Affect/Imagery/Consciousness (Vols. 1 & 2). New York, NY: Springer.

^{xxxii} Hebb, D. (1949). The Organization of Behavior: A Neuropsychological Theory. New York, NY: Wiley & Sons.

^{xxxiii} Rosenzweig, M., & Bennett, E. (1996). Psychobiology of Plasticity: Effects of Training and Experience on Brain and Behavior. *Behavioural Brain Research, 78,* 57-65.

^{xxxiv} Hebb, D. (1949). Op cit.

^{xxxv} Jenkins, J., Oatley, K., & Stein, N. (Eds.). (1998). *Human Emotions: A Reader.* Malden, MA: Blackwell Publishers, Inc., p. 8.

^{xxxvi} Greenspan, S., & Greenspan, N. (1985). *First Feelings.* New York, NY: Penguin Books, p. 8.

^{xxxvii} Oatley & Johnson-Laird, P. (1996). Op cit., p. 85.

^{xxxviii} Oatley & Johnson-Laird, P. (1996). Op cit., p. 85.

^{xxxix} Greenspan & Greenspan (1985). Op cit., pp. 4-6.

^{xl} Nathanson, D. (1993). About Emotion. Psychiatric Annals, 23 (10), p. 549.

^{xli} Ibid., p. 551, italics in the original.

^{xlii} Yarrow, L. (1961). Maternal Deprivation: Towards an Empirical and Conceptual Reevaluation. *Psychological Bulletin, 58,* p. 468.

^{xliii} Mahari, A. J. (1999). Borderline Personality from the Inside Out. Retrieved from www.borderlinepersonality.ca/borderdeeperhunger.htm, p. 1.

^{xliv} Zerbe, K. (1993). Whose Body is It Anyway? *Bulletin of the*

Menninger Clinic,57(2). Retrieved from http://www.olmo.com/psych/zerbe.htm, p. 6.

xlv Potter-Effron and Effron (1993). Op cit., p. 28.

xlvi Talbot, M. (1991). *Holographic universe*. New York, NY: Harper Collins.

xlvii Pearce, J.C. (2003). Spiritual Initiation and the Breakthrough of Consciousness: The Bond of Power. Rochester VT: Park Street Press, p. 116 and p. 115.

xlviii Turner, B. H., & Herenham, M. (1991). Thalamomygdaloid Projections in the Rat: A Test of the Amygdala's Role in Sensory Processing. *Journal of Comparative Neurology, 313*, 295-325.

xlix Zola-Morgan, S. M., & Squire, L. R. (1990). The Primate Hippocampal Formation: Evidence for a Time-Limited Role in Memory Storage. *Science, 250*, 288-290.

l Turner, B. H., & Herenham, M. (1991). Thalamomygdaloid Projections in the Rat: A Test of the Amygdala's Role in Sensory Processing. *Journal of Comparative Neurology, 313*, 295-325.

li Lynd, H. M. (1958). *On Shame and the Search for Identity*. New York, NY: Harcourt, Brace, and Company.

lii Lynd, H.M. (1958). Op cit., p. 57.

liii Armstrong, M. K. (2006). The Connection Between Shame and War. *The Journal of Psychohistory, 34*(1), p. 35.

liv Bradshaw, J. (1988b). Op cit., p. 55.

lv Nathanson, D. (1992). Op cit., p. 317.

198

^{lvi} Webb, T. (2003). Toward a Mature Shame Culture: Theoretical and Practical Tools for Personal and Social Growth. Retrieved from:

http://arrow.uws.edu.au:8080/vital/access/manager/Repository/uws:676, p. 113-114 & p. 117 Emphasis in the original.

^{lvii} Ferenczi, S. (1949). Confusion of Tongues Between the Adult and the Child. International

Journal of Psycho-Analysis, 30, p. 228.

^{lviii} Malecek, S.J. (2016a). *The Caustic Cycle of Shame.* Original published in 1998.

^{lix} Underland-Rosow, V. (1992). *The Systemic Role of Shame Within an Addictive System.* Ann Arbor MI: UMI Dissertation Services. (AAT 9223859).

^{lx} deMause, L. (1982). Op cit.

^{lxi} Miller, A. (1990). Op cit.

^{lxii} Miller, A. (1984). Op cit., p. 4.

^{lxiii} Miller, A. (1984a). Op cit.

^{lxiv} Erikson, E. (1968). *Identity, youth and crisis.* New York, NY: Norton, (p. 106, italics in the original) and p. 108.

^{lxv} Tart, C.W. (1998). Op cit.

^{lxvi} Argüelles, J. (1975). *The transformative vision.* Boulder and London: Shambhala.

^{lxvii} Potter-Effron, P. (1987). Creative Approaches to Shame and Guilt: Helping the Adult Child of an Alcoholic. *Alcoholism Treatment Quarterly, 4*, pp. 40-41.

lxviii Janoff- Bulman, R. (1985). The Aftermath of Victimization: Rebuilding Shattered Assumptions. In C. Figley (Ed.), *Trauma and its Wake: The Study and Treatment of Post-Traumatic Stress Disorder*. New York, NY: Brunner/Mazel, p. 17.

lxix Stone, A. (1992). The Role of Shame in Post-Traumatic Stress Disorder. *American Journal of Orthopsychiatry, 62*(1), p. 134.

lxx Malecek, S. J. (2009). *I am the Love I Seek*. Unpublished.

lxxi Schaler, J. (2000). *Addiction is a Choice*. Chicago, IL: Open Court.

lxxii Wolinsky, S. (1991). *Trances People Lve*. Falls Village, CT: The Bramble Company, p. 6.

lxxiii Malecek, S.J. (1998). Op cit., p. 19.

lxxiv deMause. L. (1982). Op cit.

lxxv Levenkron, S. (1998). Cutting: Understanding and Overcoming Self- Mutilation. New York, NY: W.W. Norton.

lxxvi Malecek, S.J. (1998). Op cit.

lxxvii Wolinsky, S. (1991). *Trances People Live*. Falls Village, CT: The Bramble Company, p. 6.

lxxviii Masson, J. M. (1991). *Final Analysis: The Making and Unmaking of a Psychoanalyst*. New York, NY: Harper Collins Publishing.

lxxix Freud, S. (1974). The Aetiology of Hysteria. In J. Strachey (Ed.), *Standard Edition of the Psychological Works of Sigmund Freud* (pp. 189-221). London, England: The Hogart Press & The Institute of Psychoanalysis. (Original work published 1896).
lxxx Gay, P. (1989). *The Freud Reader*. New York, NY: W.W. Norton,

p. 112.

lxxxi Kupfersmid, J. (1992). The "Defense" of Sigmund Freud. *Psychotherapy, 29*(2),

297-309.

lxxxii Colman, A. M. (2003). *Oxford Dictionary of Psychology*. Oxford, England: Oxford University Press, p. 193.

lxxxiii Meade, M. (2002). Op cit.

lxxxiv dictionary.com, accessed 01/26/17.

lxxxv Miller, A. (1990b). The Untouched Key: Tracing Childhood Trauma in Creativity and Destructiveness. New York, NY: Doubleday, pages 50, 51 & 16.

lxxxvi Colman, A.M. (2003). Op cit., p. 139.

lxxxvii Underland-Rosow, V. (1992). Op cit., p. 26.

lxxxviii Childhelp.org. (2016). CDC ACE Study (Center for Disease Control Adverse Childhood Experience. Childhelp.org. Accessed 06/08/16.

lxxxix Schwarz, A. (2015). Still in a Crib, Yet Being Given Anitpsychotics. NYT online, accessed 05/30/16.

xc Citizen Committee on Human Rights (CCHR). (2015). *Children on Psychiatric Drugs.*

https://www.cchrint.org/psychiatric-drugs/children-on-psychiatric-drugs. Accessed 05/30/16.

xci Miller, A. (1984a). Op cit., p. 4.

^{xcii} mediachannel.org, accessed 09/22/10.

^{xciii} Classen, C., Koopman, C., & Spiegel, D. (1993). Trauma and Dissociation. *Bulletin of the Menninger Clinic, 37(2)*, p. 179.

^{xciv} Wilson, R.R. (1987). Breaking the Panic Cycle: For People with Phobias. Rockville, MD: The Phobia Society of America.

^{xcv} Rossi, E.L. (1986). The Psychobiology of Mind-Body Healing: New Concepts. New York: W.W. Norton and Company.

^{xcvi} Van der Kolk, B. (1990). Op cit.

^{xcvii} Matsakis, A. (1994). Post-Traumatic Stress Disorder: A Complete Treatment Guide. 2nd Edition. Oakland CA: New Harbinger Publications, p. 53.

^{xcviii} Matsakis, A. (1994). Op cit., p. 51.

^{xcix} Briere, J., Grant-Hall, R., Pearlman, L., & Laub, D. (1992). *The Impact of Severe Trauma on the Self* [Audio Recording]. International Society of Traumatic Stress Studies, Eighth Annual Meeting, Los Angeles, CA.

^c Saunders, E., & Arnold, F. (1993). A Critique of Conceptual and Treatment Approaches to Borderline Psychopathology in Light of Findings about Childhood Abuse. *Psychiatry*, *56*, p. 192.

^{ci} Howell, E. F. (2002). Back to the "States:" Victim and Abuser States in Borderline Personality Disorder. *Psychoanalytic Dialogues, 12*, 971-986.

^{cii} Baker, R. (1998). *Child Sexual Abuse and False Memory Syndrome.* Amherst, NY: Prometheus Books, p. 231.

[ciii] Gelinas, D. (1983). The Persisting Effects of Incest. *Psychiatry, 46,* 312-32.

[civ] Cannon, W. B. (1932). *The Wisdom of the Body.* New York, NY: W.W. Norton.

[cv] Colman, A.M. (2003). Op cit., p. 279.

[cvi] Springer, J. (1994). Op. cit.

[cvii] Butler et al., (1996). Op cit., p. 49.

[cviii] Teicher, M. (2002). Scars that Won't Heal: The Neurobiology of Child Abuse. *Scientific American, 286,* 68-75.

[cix] American Psychiatric Association. (2000). Diagnostic and Statistical Manual of Mental Disorders. (4th edition—Text Revision). Washington, DC: Author, p. 519.

[cx] Browne, I. (1990). Psychological Trauma, or Unexperienced Experience. ReVision, 12, p. 33.

[cxi] Tarnopolsky, A. (2003). The Concept of Dissociation in Early Psychoanalytic Writers. *Journal of Trauma and Dissociation, 4*(3), 7-25.

[cxii] van der Kolk, B, (1990). PTSD. Symposium Conducted at the Anxiety Disorders Association of America, Tenth Annual Conference, Bethesda, Maryland.

[cxiii] Browne, I. (1990). Op cit., p. 93.

[cxiv] van der Kolk, B., as cited in Saunders, E. & Arnold, F. (1993) A Critique of Conceptual and Treatment Approaches to Borderline

Psychopathology in Light of Findings about Childhood Abuse. <u>Psychiatry</u>, <u>56</u>, 188-203.

[cxv] Butler, L., Duran, R., Jasiukaitis, P., Koopman, C., & Spiegel, D. (1996). Hypnotizability and Traumatic Experience: A Diathesis-Stress Model of Dissociative Symptomatology. *American Journal of Psychiatry, 153(7)*, July 1996 Festschrift Supplement, p. 45.

[cxvi] Lifton, R. J. (1993). *The Protean Self: Human Resilience in an Age of Fragmentation*. New York, NY: Basic Books, pp. 207-208.

[cxvii] Jourard, S. (1976). Some Ways of Unembodiment and Embodiment. *Somatics, 1*, 3-7.

[cxviii] Springer, J. (1994). Awareness, Access, and Choice: A Transpersonal Perspective on Dissociation, Association, Health and Illness. Palo Alto, CA: Institute of Transpersonal Psychology.

[cxix] Nietzche, F. (1961). *Thus Spoke Zarathustra* (R. J. Hollingdale, Trans.). New York, NY: Penguin. (Original work published 1889).

[cxx] Courtois, C. (1988). *Healing the Incest Wound*. New York, NY: Norton.

[cxxi] Colman, A.M. (2003). Op cit., p. 588.

[cxxii] Friere as cited in Albert et al., (1986), Op. cit., p. 6.

[cxxiii] Ibid., p. 81.

[cxxiv] Talbot, M. (1991). Op cit.,

[cxxv] Tart, C.W. (1988). Op cit., p. 8.

[cxxvi] Springer, J. (1994). Op cit., p. 76-77.

[cxxvii] Stone, H., & Stone, S. (1989). *Embracing Ourselves*. San Rafael,

CA: New World Library, p. 13.

cxxviii Springer, J. (1994). Op cit., p. 7 and p. 3.

cxxix Richards, D. G. (1990). Dissociation and Transformation. *Journal of Humanistic Psychology, 30*, p. 54.

cxxx Ross, C. (1991). Op cit., p. 56.

cxxxi Colman, A.M. (2003). Op cit., p. 12.

cxxxii Kasl, C. (1989). *Women, Sex and Addiction.* New York, NY: Harper and Row, p. 15.

cxxxiii Bradshaw, J. (1988b). Op cit., p. 96.

cxxxiv Szasz, T. (1994). *Cruel Compassion.* Syracuse, NY: Syracuse University Press as cited in Schaler (2000), Op cit., p. 15 and p. 16.

cxxxv Bardo, M., Donohew, R., & Harrington, N. (1996). Psychophysiology of Novelty Seeking and Drug Seeking Behavior. *Behavioural Brain Research 77*, p. 23.

cxxxvi King County Bar Project. (2005). (KCBP). Retrieved from http://www.kcba.org/druglaw/pdf/EffectiveDrugControl.pdf.

cxxxvii Malecek, S. J. (2002). Ideological Hegemony, Childrearing, Shame, and Health. Unpublished manuscript.

cxxxviii Davies, J.B. (1997). Op cit., P. 15.

cxxxix Peele, S. (1998). Op cit., pp. 156-157.

cxl Peele, S. (1998). *Diseasing of America.* San Francisco, CA: Josey-Bass, p. 129.

cxli Peele, S. (1998). Op cit., p. 31-32.

205

[cxlii] Schaler, J. (2000). Op cit., PP 4-5.

[cxliii] Kasl, C. (1989). Op cit., p. 28.

[cxliv] Schaler, J. (2000). Op cit., p. 128.

[cxlv] Nathanson, D. (1993). Op cit., p. 544.

[cxlvi] Schaler, J. (2000). Op cit., p. 9.

[cxlvii] Peele, S. (1998). Op cit., p. 26.

[cxlviii] Ibid., p. 144 and p. xvii.

[cxlix] Schaler, J. ((2000). Op cit., p. 7.

[cl] Ibid.

[cli] Diamond, J. (1989). *The adrenaline Addict*. San Rafael, CA: Author.

[clii] Malecek, S.J. (1998). Op cit.

[cliii] Ibid.

[cliv] Reed, L. (1969). *Heroin: The Velvet Underground and Nico*. Hollywood, CA: Polydor.

[clv] Jung, C.G. (1966). Paracelsus, 3-12, in CW 15: The Spirit in Man, Art, and Literature. RFC Huck (tr.) Princeton NJ: Princeton University Press, p. 4. (Original work published in 1929).

[clvi] Colman, A.M. (2003). Op cit., p. 716.

[clvii] Rankin, I. (1988). The watchman. London UK: Bodley Head, p. 8.

[clviii] Pearce, J.C. (2003). Op. cit.

[clix] Glendinning, C. (1994). My Name is Chellis and I'm in Recovery from Western Civilization. Boston, MA: Shambhala, p. 87.

clx Chomsky, N. (2015). Requiem for the American Dream. IMDb Productions.

clxi qz.com. (2012). Brazil now consumes 18% of the world's cocaine. http://qz.com/5058/brazil-now-consumes-18%-of-worlds-cocaine. Accessed 06/01/16.

clxii U.S. Department of Health & Human Services. (2012). Substance Abuse—A National Challenge: Prevention, Treatment, and Research at HHS. Retrieved from http:///Substance-Abuse/Substance-Abuse-A-National-Challenge-Prevention-Treatment-and-Research-at-HHS/article/6445/1.html.

clxiii Office of National Drug Control Policy. (2007). https://www.ncjrs.gov/pdffiles1/ondcp/216431.pdf. P. 23.

clxiv Schaler, J. (2000). Op cit., p. XVI (emphasis in the original).

clxv Roszak, T. (1969). The Making of a Counterculture. Berkeley CA: University of California Press.

clxvi McLean, I. (2009). The Concise Oxford Dictionary of Politics. Oxford University: Oxford University Press, p. 490.

clxvii Darwin, C. (1859). On the Origin of Species by Means of Natural Selection, or the Preservation of Favoured Races in the Struggle for Life" John Murray: London, UK.

clxviii Mayr, E. (1982). The Growth of Biological Thought. Cambridge MA: Harvard University Press, pp. 479-480.

clxix Seligman, M. (1975). Op cit.

clxx Miller, A. (1984a). Op cit., p. 58.

clxxi Althusser (cited in Boggs, C. [1989]. *Social Movements and Political Power*. Philadelphia, PA: Temple University Press.

clxxii Anderson, W.T. (1990). *Reality isn't what it used to be*. San Francisco, CA: Harper & Row, p. 116.

clxxiii Chomsky, N. (as cited in Wintonick, P., & Achbar, M. (1994). *Manufacturing Consent: Noam Chomsky and the media*. New York, NY: Black Rose Books, p. 43.

clxxiv Albert et al. (1986). Op cit., p. 20.

clxxv Berger & Luckmann (1967). Op cit., p. 121.

clxxvi Lopes, C. (1991). Op cit., p. 2.

clxxvii Dictionary.com. Greed. Accessed 12/18/12.

clxxviii Schmookler, A. B. (1984). *The Parable of the Tribes*. Boston, MA: Houghton Mifflin Company

clxxix Tolle, E. (2006). *A New Earth*. New York, NY: Dunlop.

clxxx Potter-Effron & Effron. (1993). Op. cit., p. 28.

clxxxi Kavanaugh, J. (1990). Op cit., p. 304.

clxxxii Wilber, K. (1995). *Sex, Ecology, Spirituality*. Boston, MA: Shambhala.

clxxxiii Howard, J. A., & Hollander, J. (2000). *Gendered Situations, Gendered Selves*. Walnut Creek, CA: Altamira Press, p. 60.

clxxxiv Gold, S. (2004). Op cit., p. 31.

clxxxv Horn, K. (2005). The North American holocaust. In Stalinist Espresso,

Genocide. Espressostalinust.com (accessed May 12, 2010).

clxxxvi Hansi, L. W. Broken Promises on display at Native American Treaties exhibit. npr.org/sections/codeswitch/2015/01/18/368559990 (accessed 05/22/16).

clxxxvii Albert et al. (1986). Op cit., p. 65.

clxxxviii Henry, J. (1963). *Culture Against Man*. New York, NY: Random House, pp. 105-106.

clxxxix Schumaker, J. F. (2001). *The Age of Insanity: Modernity and Mental Health*. Westport, CT: Praeger Publishers, p. 17.

cxc Tart, C.W. (1988). Op cit.

cxci Henry, J. (1963). Op cit., p. 19, p. 25, and p. 70.

cxcii Ibid., p. 47, p. 55, and p. 95.

cxciii Chomsky (as cited in Wintock & Achbar, 1994), Op cit., p. 43

cxciv Wolinsky, S. (1991). Op cit., p. 3.

cxcv Brookfield, S. (1987). *Developing Critical Thinking*. San Francisco, CA: Jossey-Bass.

cxcvi Argüelles, J. (1975). Op cit., p. 279 and p. 277.

cxcvii Foffman (as cited in Howard & Hollander), Op. cit., p. 100.

cxcviii Howard & Hollander. (2000). Op. cit., p. 98.

cxcix Ibid., p. 98.

cc Laing, R.D. (1959). Op cit.

cci Mander, J. (1977). Four Arguments for the Elimination of Television. New ork, NY: Quill.

[ccii] Moore, W. (2001). Television: Opiate of the Masses. *Journal of Cognitive Liberties, 2*(2), 59-66.

[cciii] Gelles, R., & Strauss, M. (1988). *Intimate Violence.* New York, NY: Simon and Schuster Touchstone Books, p. 197.

[cciv] Breggin, P. (1991). *Toxic Psychiatry.* New York, NY: St. Martin's Press.

[ccv] Springer, J. (1994). Op cit.

[ccvi] Butler et al. (1996). Op cit.

[ccvii] Van der Kolk (as cited in Saunders and Arnold. (1993). Op cit.

[ccviii] Newsome, J.S. (2015). *The Mask You Live In.* The Representation Project.

[ccix] NYT online. NYT.com, 08/25/13, accessed 01/21/17.

[ccx] Clarke, A.C. (1973). Profiles of the Future. 2nd Ed. New York: Harper & Row, p. 21, fn. 1).

[ccxi] Means, R. (2012). If You've Forgotten the Names of the Clouds, You've Lost Your Way. Porcupine SD & Santa Monica CA: Treaty Publications, p. 29.

[ccxii] Glendenning, C. (1994). Op cit.,

[ccxiii] Ibid., p. 77 and p. 64.

[ccxiv] Burdett, J. (2010). Godfather of Kathmandu. New York: Alfred A. Knopf, p. 192.

[ccxv] Rao, V. (2011). A Brief History of the Corporation 1600-1800. ribbonfarm.com 06/08/11. (Accessed: 05/19/16).

ccxvi Hosmer, J. K. (1988). *James Adams: Facts on File, Inc.* New York, NY: Houghton-Mifflin, p. 212.

ccxvii Rao, V. (2011). Op. cit.

ccxviii Horowitz, M. (1977). *Transformation of American Law (Studies in Legal History) 1780-1860.* Cambridge, MA: Harvard University Press, p. 12.

ccxix Hinkley, R. (2004, September). Twenty-eight Words that Could Change the World. *Sun Magazine, 345*, p. 9.

ccxx Bellotti, 435 U.S. at 809. White, J., Dissenting (as cited in Grossman, Linzey, & Brannen, 2003).

ccxxi Korten, D. (2007, September). Everybody Wants to Rule the World. *Sun*

Magazine, 381, p. 7.

ccxxii Mander, G. (1991). Op cit.

ccxxiii Lopes, C. (1990). Op cit., p.3.

ccxxiv Bellotti, Op. cit.

ccxxv As cited in Grossman et al. (2003). Op. cit.

ccxxvi Kennedy, D. (2003, May 2). Silent Swoosh. *Boston Phoenix.* Retrieved from: http://www.bostonphoenix.com/boston/news_features/dont_quote _me/multi-page/documents/02860571.htm.

ccxxvii Santa Clara Co. v. Railroad Company, (as cited in Grossman et al., 2003).

ccxxviii (as cited in Grossman et al., 2003).

ccxxix Wikepedia, accessed April 30, 2015.

ccxxx Scott, R. (2011) Heading South: U.S.-Mexico Trade and Job Displacement after NAFTA. Washington DC: Economic Policy Institute, May 3, 2011, p. 1-3.

ccxxxi Anderson, W.T. (1990). Op cit., p. 123.

ccxxxii Mander, J. (1977). Four Arguments for the Elimination of Television. New York, NY: Quill.

ccxxxiii Anderson, W.T. (1990). Op cit., p. 126.

ccxxxiv Hertsgaard, M. (1989). *On Bended Knee*. New York, NY: Schocken Books, p. 19-20.

ccxxxv Dave Manuel.com. accessed 5/14/16.

ccxxxvi wasingtonpost.com, accessed 01/24/17.

ccxxxvii Korten, D. (2007, September). Everybody Wants to Rule the World. *Sun Magazine, 381,* p. 8.

ccxxxviii Ibid., p. 8.

ccxxxix Ibid., p. 9.

ccxl Malkin, J. (2006). And a Time for Peace: Kathy Kelly Puts Herself in Harm's Way to Oppose War. *Sun Magazine, 362*, pp. 4-13.

ccxli The Sentencing Project (2014), p. 128, accessed 08/12/14.

ccxlii Kelley, H.H. (1967). Attribution Theory in Social Psychology. In D. Levine (Ed.), Nebraska symposium on motivation, pp. 192-238. Lincoln: University of Nebraska Press.

ccxliii Korten, D. (2007). Op cit., p. 7.

ccxliv Hinkley, R. (2004). Op cit., p. 11.

ccxlv   https://www.dailyinfographic.com/the-stats-on-internet-pornography-infographic.com, p. 2.

ccxlvi Korten, D. (2007). Op cit.

ccxlvii Diamond, J. (1989). Op cit., p. 19.

ccxlviii Ibid., p. 31 and p. 32.

ccxlix Ibid., p. 32 and p. 35

ccl Grof, S. (1985). Op cit., p. 85.

ccli Ibid., p. 316 & p. 318.

cclii Szasz, T. (1974). Op cit., p. 12.

ccliii Ibid., p. 85.

ccliv Breggin, P. (1991). *Toxic Psychiatry*. New York, NY: St. Martin's Press, pp. 24-25, & p. 27.

cclv Grof, S. (1985). Op cit., p. 143

cclvi Gay, P. (1989). *The Freud reader*. New York, NY: W.W. Norton, p. 1 12.

cclvii APA. (2000). Op cit., p. 467.

cclviii Masson, J. M. (1991). *Final Analysis: The Making and Unmaking of a Psychoanalyst*. New York, NY: Harper Collins Publishing, pp. 208-209.

cclix Grof, S. (1985). Op cit., p.324.

cclx Ibid., p. 5.

cclxi Wilber, K. (2001). *Eye to Eye: Quest for a New Paradigm*. Boston, MA: Shambhala, p. 16.

cclxii Szasz, T. (1974). Op cit., p. 2, and p. vii.

cclxiii Howard & Hollander. (2000). Op cit., p. 49.

cclxiv Glendenning, C. (1994). Op cit., p. xiii.

cclxv Ibid., p. 8.

cclxvi Ibid., P. 5

cclxvii Wilber, K. (2000). Op cit., p. ix.

cclxviii Illich, I. (1976). *Medical Nemesis: The Expropriation of Health*. New York, NY: Random House, p. 6.

cclxix Szasz, T. (1963). *Law, Liberty and Psychiatry*. New York, NY: Collier Books, pp. 79-80.

cclxx Ibid., p. 14 & pp. 16-17.

cclxxi Szasz, T. (1974). Op cit., p. xii and p. x.

cclxxii Szasz, T. (1963). Op cit., p. 13.

cclxxiii Szasz, T. Ibid., p. xi.

cclxxiv Wilber, K. (1995; 2000). Op. cit.

cclxxv Breggin, P. (1991). Op cit., p. 22-23.

cclxxvi Ibid., pp. 55-56 (emphasis in the original); and p. 59.

cclxxvii Harrison, E. (1962). Rockefeller Gives Long-Term Plan for Mental Care. <u>New York Times</u>, January 31, 1962, (cited in CCHR). (1999).Op cit., p. 1.

[cclxxviii] Menninger, W., cited in Wiseman, B. (1995), pp. 105-107. *Psychiatry: The Ultimate Betrayal*. Los Angeles, CA: Freedom Publishers.

[cclxxix] Szasz, T. (1994). *Cruel Compassion*. Syracuse, NY: Syracuse University Press, p. 160.

[cclxxx] Grof, S. (1985). Op cit., p. 318.

[cclxxxi] U.S. Department of Health. (1987). *U.S. Mental Health Budget*. Washington, DC: Author, p. 56.

[cclxxxii] U.S. Department of Health. (1998). *U.S. Mental Health Budget*. Washington, DC: Author, p. 162.

[cclxxxiii] Ibid., p. 357.

[cclxxxiv] CCHR, (1999), p. 1.

[cclxxxv] Sharkey, J. (1994). Bedlam: *Greed, Profiteering and Fraud, a Mental Health System Gone Crazy*. New York: St. Martin's Press, p. 175.

[cclxxxvi] U.S. Department of Health & Human Services. (2005). Substance Abuse—A National Challenge: Prevention, Treatment, and Research at HHS. Retrieved from http:///Substance-Abuse/Substance-Abuse-A-National-Challenge-Prevention-Treatment-and-Research-at-HHS/article/6445/1.html.

[cclxxxvii] Goode, E. (1999, June 15). Tireless, Outspoken and Atypical, Mental Health Chief Rocks the Boat. Retrieved from http://www.nytimes.com/1999/06/15/health/scientist-work-steve-hyman-tireless-outspoken-atypical-mental-health-chief-rocks.html, p. 1.

[cclxxxviii] Sharkey, J. (1994). Op cit., p. 240.

cclxxxix Angell, cited in Latham, 2011, p. 1).

ccxc Grof, S. (1985). Op cit., p. 319.

ccxci Kaiser, D. (1996). Commentary Against Biologic Psychiatry. Retrieved from http://www.evolver.net/user/the_sanctuary_at_sedonacom/blog/myth_ch emical_imbalancewww.mhsource.com/edu/psytimes/p961242.html, para 9.1.

ccxcii The Great Waste. http://psychfraud.freedommag.org/page04a.htm (retrieved February 7, 2016).

ccxciii Harris, G. (2009). Drug Makers are Advocacy Group's Biggest Donors. New York Times, October 21, 2009. www.nytimes.com. Accessed October 8, 2010.

ccxciv Breggin, P. (1991) Op. cit., pp. 344-345.

ccxcv Masson, J.M. (1991). Op cit.

ccxcvi Flaccus, Q. H. (23 BCE). *Odes: Book III.* Rome, Italy: Unknown.

ccxcvii Schmookler, A.B. (1988). Op cit.

ccxcviii Harvard Law Review. (1903). *Respondeat Superior.* Harvard Law School: Cambridge MA. pp 51-52.

ccxcix Colman, A.M (2003). Op cit., p. 588.

ccc Keen, S. (1986). *Faces of the Enemy: Reflections of the Hostile Imagination.* San Francisco, CA: Harper & Row Publishers.

ccci Keen, S. (1986). Op cit.

cccii Schmookler, A. B. (1988*). Out of Weakness: Healing the Wounds that Drive Us to War.* New York, NY: Bantam Books, p. 210-211.

[ccciii] Schmookler, A.B. (1988). Op cit., p. 233.

[ccciv] O'Sullivan, J. (1845/1939). "Annexation," *United States Magazine and Democratic Review 17,* No. 1 (July-August 1845): pp. 5-10.

[cccv] Schmookler, A.B. (1988). Op cit., p. 236.

[cccvi] Bowlby, J. (1983). Op cit.

[cccvii] Miller, A. (1990). Op cit., p. 4.

[cccviii] Mitscherlich, A., & Mitscherlich, M. (1975). *The Inability to Mourn.* New York, NY: Grove Press.

[cccix] Schmookler, A.B. (1988). Op cit., p. 222.

[cccx] Nathansom, D. (1994). Op cit.

[cccxi] Chomsky, N. (2004). Op cit., p. 74.

[cccxii] Chomsky, N., Mitchell, P., & Schoeffel, J. (2002). *Understanding Power.* New York, NY: The New Press, p. 56.

[cccxiii] Keen, S. (1986). Op cit.

[cccxiv] Herman & Chomsky. (1988). Op cit., p. 350.

[cccxv] Gold, S. (2004). Op cit., p. 31.

[cccxvi] Chomsky, N., Mitchell, P., & Schoeffel, J. (2002). *Understanding Power.* New York, NY: The New Press, p. 56.

[cccxvii] Schmookler, A.B. (1988). Op cit., p. 208.

[cccxviii] Scheer, R. (2001). *Bush's Faustian Deal with the Taliban.* LA Times. May 23rd, 2001, p. 1. http://www.workingforchange.com/article.cpm?ItemID=1152.

[cccxix] Shainberg, D. (1987). Vortices of Thought in the Implicate Order.

In B. Hiley & F. D. Peat (Eds.), *Quantum Implications* (pp. 396-414). New York, NY: Routledge & Kegan Paul, p. 402.

cccxx Lopes, C. (1990). Op cit., p. 1.

cccxxi Ibid., p. 4.

cccxxii McLaughlin, C., & Catania, S. (1991, February, 27). Editor and publisher. *San Francisco Bay Guardian*, p. 12.

cccxxiii Kleveman, L. (2004, February 16). Oil and the New 'Great Game.' *The Nation*, p. 11.

cccxxiv Miller, S. (1969). Space Cowboy. Brave New World. Los Angeles: Capitol Records.

cccxxv Sussman, H. (1997). The Aesthetic Contract: Statues of Art and Intellectual Work In Modernity. Palo Alto: Stanford University Press, p. 42.

cccxxvi Schmookler, A.B. (1988). Op cit., p. 222.

cccxxvii Diamond, J. (1989). Op cit., p. 12.

cccxxviii Henry, J. (1963). Op cit., p. 102.

cccxxix Henry, J. (1963). Op cit., p. 263.

cccxxx Glendenning, C. (1994). Op cit., pp. 21-22.

cccxxxi Wordsworth, W. (1806). Ode: Intimations of Immortality *from Recollections of Early Childhood*. Couch, A. Q. (1919). Ed., The Oxford Book of English Verse: pp. 1250–1900. Public Domain, lines 59-66.

cccxxxii Fornari, F. (1966). *The Psychoanalysis of War*. Garden City, NY: Auction Books, p. 51.

cccxxxiii Lynd, H.M. (1958). *On Shame and the Search for Identity*. New York, NY: Harcourt, Brace, and Company, p. 57.

cccxxxiv Piers & Singer. (1953). Op cit., p. 150.

cccxxxv Potter-Effron, P. (1987). Creative Approaches to Shame and Guilt: Helping the Adult Child of an Alcoholic. *Alcoholism Treatment Quarterly, 4*, 41-42.

cccxxxvi Bradshaw, J. (1988b). Op. cit., p.190.

cccxxxvii (dictionary.com, accessed 01/27/17).

cccxxxviii Blavatsky, H.P. (1962/1889). The Key to Theosophy. Pasadena CA: Theosophical Society Press, p. 17.

cccxxxix I Ching. (1980). *Book of Changes*. Richard Wilhelm (tr. From Chinese into   German); Cary F. Baynes (tr. From German into English). Princeton NJ: Princeton University Press. (Original edition published 1950), Hexagram 28, p. 112.

cccxl Nietzche, F. (1961). *Thus Spoke Zarathustra* (R. J. Hollingdale, Trans.).   New York, NY: Penguin. (Original work published 1889).

cccxli Plato (360 BCE), as cited in Sedley, 2003, p. 6, & pp. 13-14.

cccxlii Freud, S. (1965). *The interpretation of dreams*. New York: Avon, 1965, p. 483. (Original work published 1900).

cccxliii dictionary.com, accessed 01/27/17.

cccxliv Schmookler, A.B. (1988). Op cit., p. 235).

cccxlv Dictionary.com (accessed 03/28/15).

cccxlvi Jung, C. G. (1936). Psychology and Religion, in CW 11:

Psychology and Religion: East and West. Princeton: Princeton University Press, p. 131.

cccxlvii Miller, A. (1990a). Op cit., p. 131 and p. 50.

cccxlviii Shay, J. (1994). Achilles in Viet Nam: Combat trauma and the undoing of character. New York: Scribner, p. 187.

cccxlix Colman, A. M. (2003). Op. cit., p. 3.

cccl Malouin, Paul-Jacques. (1751). "Alchemy." The Encyclopedia of Diderot & d'Alembert. Collaborative Translation Project. Translated by Lauren Yoder. Ann Arbor: Michigan Publishing, University of Michigan Library, 2003. Web. [accessed 05/13/15]]. <http://hdl.handle.net/2027/spo.did2222.0000.057. Trans. of "Alchimie," Encyclopédie ou Dictionnaire raiso nné des sciences, des arts et des métiers, vol. 1. Paris.

cccli Shay, J. (1994). Op. cit., pp. 188-189.

ccclii Shay, J. (1994). Op. cit., p. 63.

cccliii Frey, WH 2nd, DeSota-Johnson, D., Hoffman, C., & McCall JT. Effect of stimulus on the chemical composition of human tears. Am J Ophthalmology. 1981 Oct; 92(4):559-67.

cccliv Anderson, R. (1996). Nine psycho-spiritual characteristics of spontaneous and

involuntary weeping. Journal of Transpersonal Psychology, 28 (2), 43-49.

ccclv Nin, A. (1974). Diary of Anais Nin. Volume 5, 1947-1955. Chicago: Swallow Press.

[ccclvi] Herlong & Herlong. (1995). Op. cit., p. v.

[ccclvii] Argüelles, J. (1975). Op cit., p. 275.

[ccclviii] Dekker, J. (1990). Crisis in Belief Systems. In *An Interdisciplinary Approach to the World and its Discontents seminar*. San Francisco, CA: New College of California. Speaker.

[ccclix] Shaw, G.B. (1907). Major Barbara. London UK: Archibald Constable & Company.

[ccclx] Fromm, E. (1968). The revolution of hope. New York: Harper and Row, p. 80.

[ccclxi] Roszak, T. (1992). *The Voice of the Earth*. New York, NY: Simon & Schuster, p. 302.

[ccclxii] Wilber, K. (1995). Op cit., p. 9 and p. 10.

[ccclxiii] Lovejoy, A. (1964/1936). The great chain of being. Cambridge: Harvard University Press, p. 26.

[ccclxiv] Wilber, K. (2001). Op cit., p. 65.

[ccclxv] Sahtouris, E. (1989). Gaia: The Human Journey from Chaos to Cosmos. New York,

NY: Pocket Books.

[ccclxvi] Wilber, K. (1983/1990). Op cit., p. 5.

[ccclxvii] Wilber, K. (1995). Op cit., p. 19.

[ccclxviii] Mander, G. (1991). Op cit., p. 65 and p. 379.

[ccclxix] Argüelles, J. (1975). Op cit., p. 278.

[ccclxx] Wilber, K. (2000). Op cit., p. 238.

221

ccclxxi Johnson, D. (1975). The Body, the Cathedral and the Kiva. In D. Joffe (Ed.), *In Search of Therapy*. New York, NY: Harper and Row, p. 142.

ccclxxii Bohm, D. (1990). The implicate order. *Clarion Call 3*(3), p. 34.

ccclxxiii Bradshaw, J. (1992). *Creating Love: The Next Great Stage of Growth*. New York, NY: Bantam Books, p. 336.

ccclxxiv Argüelles, J. (1975). Op cit., p. 287.

ccclxxv Roszak, T. (1992). Op cit., p. 302.

ccclxxvi Gold, S. (2004). Op cit., p. 15.

ccclxxvii Bradshaw, J. (1992). Op cit., p. 346.

ccclxxviii Gottner-Abendroth, H. (1986). Nine Principles of a Matriarchal Aesthetic. In G.Ecker (Ed.), & H. Anderson (Trans.), *Feminist Aesthetics*, p. 86. Boston, MA: Beacon Press.

ccclxxix Chang, C. (1970). *Creativity and Taoism*. New York, NY: Harper Colophon Books, p. 38.

Made in the USA
Columbia, SC
17 May 2020